CW00689975

THE ENTREPRENEU
TO A GOOD NIGHT'S SLEEP

For a complete list of Management Books 2000 titles
visit our web-site on http://www.mb2000.com

THE ENTREPRENEUR'S GUIDE TO A GOOD NIGHT'S SLEEP

Michael Bell

2000

First published in 2007 by Management Books 2000 Ltd
Forge House, Limes Road
Kemble, Cirencester
Gloucestershire, GL7 6AD, UK
Tel: 0044 (0) 1285 771441
Fax: 0044 (0) 1285 771055
Email: info@mb2000.com
Web: www.mb2000.com

Printed and bound in Great Britain by 4edge Ltd of Hockley, Essex – www.4edge.co.uk

British Library Cataloguing in Publication Data is available

IBN 9781852525705

Acknowledgements

I would like to thank Glen McCoy, my personal coach and mentor whose coaching and help have been invaluable throughout the years.

Also a thank you to my office manager Helen Sweet who has been dedicated to the cause, having listened with enthusiasm to my ramblings and dreams and never doubting me through the past eleven years.

I would also give a big thank you to all the *Results Financial* team, each and every one of them for their part in the growth of *Results Financial*.

Finally to all the caring and dedicated people I have had the pleasure of knowing and working with through the Financial Services industry, including all my clients.

To my wife Pam, my daughter Mandy and my Mum and Dad.
All of whom in their own way inspired me to achieve.
I just wish my Dad was still around to have seen this book
published.

Contents

Foreword

It is only after reading Mike Bell's fascinating insight into the achievement of success in business, and indeed in life, that the blinding logic of this book's intriguing title strikes home.

A successful businessman and a delightful individual in his own right it has been my privilege to have known Mike for a number of years. It is typical of his willingness to help others and share ideas that he should put together such an eminently useful yet readable guide to success.

I know from personal experience the impact such a book can have on one's life, having had my own journey through life transformed almost 50 years ago by something as "simple" as a handful of chapters in an inspirational guide to success.

"Purpose, deadline and passion" are Mike's watchwords for the achievement of success as an entrepreneur and you will find them present in abundance in this incredibly practical guide to business success.

As Michael Bell says, "Buy It! If you think you don't need it perhaps its time to forget about creating a business and get yourself a job!"

Ken Davy
Chairman
Simply Biz

Introduction

Were you aware that eighty percent of all new enterprises fail within the first year?

Okay, that's not the most inspirational way to start a book on business success, and I want to put this piece of information up in lights because whilst it's true it doesn't mean that you have to be part of the sad majority of this statistic.

A while back I went to my doctor with a pain in my shoulder. He explained to me that it might be a frozen shoulder and for someone of my age the chances of the frozen shoulder completely recovering was five in a hundred.

"That's great news," I said when I heard it and watched him look up at me in surprise.

"What's great about that?"

"I'll be one of the five percent," I replied.

"No, you don't understand – you can't choose to be one of the five percent," he said, and for the first time my doctor was looking at me as if I was also suffering with some mental delusion whilst I was viewing having someone like him a bit of a liability and was even contemplating finding someone new.

Before you get completely the wrong idea about this book, may I assure you that if you have a number of solid beliefs that you are not prepared to take a really close look at, this book is not for you. You will be wasting your time, energy and money.

If on the other hand you are about to start a business or already own a small or medium-sized enterprise and you're looking for help, inspiration and a few tips to take your achievement to a higher place, then I respectfully invite you to read on and I will deem it a genuine privilege to share what I can with you through these thirteen chapters.

When I first spoke to my publisher about this project, he tried to get me to classify it. Was it a business self-help book, a motivational piece for small businesses, or a practical how-to-do-it book on some specific aspect of running a small business?

I suppose it's all of these things and yet none of these things. In fact, I'm going to ask you to make your own decision on its classification after you've read it. Indeed, I would be delighted to hear from you and any feedback would be much appreciated. My email address is at the end of this introduction.

Another conversation I had with my publisher revolved around the fact that there are hundreds of thousands of books around running a small business out there. A fairly legitimate question was quite simply: "Does the world need another book on the subject?"

I think this will be particularly of value to you if you do run or are intending to start up your own small business. If you're someone who doesn't have a business background or any formal qualification or training around running a business, then I would feel really honoured if this is the first book that gets you on your way to ultimate success.

Another reason for my writing this is that when I first started out myself there weren't too many simple-to-read and digest books available. There were scores of books detailing the technicalities and practicalities of setting up a small business, and formal tomes written by highly qualified MBAs detailing the ins and outs of what they deem is the route to success, none of which seemed to hit the spot.

At this point I must raise my hands and declare that I am not a master of business administration and apart from some personal coaching around business success, I have never undertaken any formal training on the subject. I have to say that this was probably the best thing that ever happened to me in relation to achieving my own ultimate success. Where I would never decry anyone wishing to study business subjects, I would like to point out at this very early stage that business success is twenty percent business technique and eighty percent mindset management.

In fact, I have never known any really successful person in business ever start with a formal course in running a small business, which ultimately led them to growing their own massively successful operation or world-class business success. When you think of people like Richard Branson (Virgin), the late Anita Roddick (The Body Shop) and Ray Kroc (McDonald's) you are also instantly aware that their achievements happened largely as a result of what they thought, and had little to do with formal business education. Now, if you can have it both ways, then I salute you – and equally, if you haven't the time or inclination to go down the formal route, I am simply saying that you can still achieve unlimited success.

My own chosen business lies in the arena of financial services and I am delighted to say that my company, *Results Financial*, is currently one of the most successful financial services consultancies of its size in the UK. Yet this book is not about financial services nor is it a guide to create a financial services consulting firm.

I hope you will discover that it's much more exciting than anything so specific and that the concepts and ideas that I am now about to share with you may be applied not only to a business, new or existing, but also to life itself. There's also nothing particularly unusual about me nor did I have any unfair advantages when I started my company. In fact, I began it on a shoestring budget, a handful of ideals and one very specific goal.

In April 1998 I decided to create a business process, or dare I say business product in its own right, that I could construct, continue to build and one day, should I choose to, sell or pass on to those key individuals who had helped me create its success.

What I set out to achieve was not about having a business; it was about attaining my freedom by using a business as a bridge between where I was and where I wanted to be.

Let me also say that for the word 'business' you may substitute 'novel', 'movie', 'media product' or 'art form'.

I would like to share with you my objectives for creating this book in the first place.

Firstly, I would like to give away all my discoveries. As I am writing this I was tempted to use the word 'secrets' and yet it's not about secrets because the discoveries I made were all staring me in the face. It's just that very often we overlook the obvious and attempt to seek out little-known concepts believing that they have more value attached to them. I think it's general knowledge these days that in business particularly, it's the simple things or ideas that achieve the greatest success and it's also the small things that make the biggest difference. So it's simple and small versus big, convoluted and complex.

Secondly, I would really like to smash a few paradigms for you. As you're probably aware, a paradigm is an accepted belief or set of beliefs that you're probably reluctant to change (strictly, an assumed pattern or 'model' describing your business approach). Some paradigms can be in your best interest, whilst the ones I wish to get rid of are those beliefs and ideas that hold you back, often where you are completely ignorant of the true facts. There are lots of paradigms involved in running a business, though I must ask you to take full responsibility in deciding on those you wish to keep and those you wish to remove or change. Some of the business myths or paradigms include:

- **A business is difficult to set up.**

- **Successful business often takes a long period before any returns are forthcoming.**

- **One of the biggest challenges in business is the competition.**

- **You have to be qualified or experienced to run a business.**

- **A successful business is normally operated by an entrepreneur who has had their fair share of luck.**

Lastly, I wanted to write a book that would pay back the debt I owe so many different people. I refer to those individuals who've really been a source of inspiration and support without whom I may have floundered and fallen. To these people: I salute you and dedicate this book to you. I also hope that this book will trigger new and highly successful businesses which in turn trigger lots of other new and refreshing books on similar subjects.

Whoever you are and whatever you desire from these pages, may I wish you every success.

Michael Bell, 2007
mbell@resultsfinancial.co.uk

**Aim for the moon.
If you miss, you may hit a star.**

W. Clement Stone

1

Taking the Plunge

Walk down any high street, into a shopping centre, on to a business park or hub of commercial excellence and take a moment. Take a long hard look at the nearest business before you, and, whether or not you're in business yourself, think about the decisions that were made to create the spectacle you are now looking at. Some of the decisions will have been good ones – perhaps reflected in successful well-known brands. If the business is successful, you might conclude that whoever the creative genius was behind the decisions, he (or she) obviously made some good ones.

Then there are those *unknown* businesses which make up by far the majority of enterprises. They are either in a start-up phase or in a gentle decline. Someone probably made some poor decisions in *their* creation or current management.

It's not quite a decade since I made a start with my current business, and I do know it was a big decision whether or not to take the plunge. I had several conversations with family members, friends and a couple of professionals. Fortunately I made the right decision, yet isn't it interesting how many people never start the business they've always wanted because they're daunted by the decision-making process?

Mind management in decision-making

From my own experience I know that one of the most daunting things for anyone in making good decisions is managing their thoughts so that the decision emerges based on having the ability to sift through those elements of the decision-making process that are relevant versus the other aspects which are irrelevant.

So often we're crowded in our thinking by various red herrings. Certainly in my own business I've discovered that the two maxims 'less is more' and 'simplicity over complexity' have won the day time and time again in achieving the right decision. I always remember the well-known matchbox story – the one about the Swan Vesta company, who managed to save a vast amount of money by removing one side of sandpaper from all their matchboxes. Up until that point, they used to manufacture each box of matches with two sides of sandpaper to strike the match. It took a bright spark in their organisation to rationalise that there was no need for this unnecessary additional expense. It subsequently made a big difference to their bottom line.

The following aide-memoire was once given to me, and I now have it taped inside my paper diary:

The 10 Keys to Making Any Decision

1. **State the task and the main objective.**

2. **Clarify if there are other people involved.**

3. **Is there a bigger picture that's been overlooked?**

4. **Break the way forward into 'bite-sized pieces'.**

5. **Who is going to do what? Is it do-able now?**

6. **Balance the 'risk versus reward'.**

7. **Think of the impact success will bring.**

8. **Think of the worst thing that could happen – is this an issue in reality?**

9. **Make the decision!**

10. **Take action.**

Decisions can depend on set beliefs. So often in running a small business we allow ourselves to be governed by these paradigms or beliefs set in stone that have been foisted upon us purely because it appears to be the accepted way.

These beliefs are invariably other people's beliefs, and as a bit of a rebel, I often completely refute traditional ideas if they stop me in my tracks from achieving the outcome I am looking for. Of course there has to be integrity in place at all times, but that aside why do entrepreneurs allow themselves to be short-changed by other people's insecurities?

So what's the journey with this book?

I suppose it's time to lay my cards on the table. This book has a very specific purpose. Now I could spill all the beans now and lay it out before you, or save something quite mind-blowing for later. My decision is a half way measure: to tell you what you need to know now, and then check back with you nearer the end to see if you've benefited from my primary objective in writing this book.

Suffice to say, I am eager to make a difference to you. If after you've read this cover to cover, you feel you have really got the point, I would love to hear from you. I'm in the phone book at *Results Financial* in Sheffield. And if you've read it and not got the point – then I think there may be more of a reason to get in touch! Either way, I am viewing you as someone about to take the plunge with their business, or someone already running their own SME (small to medium size enterprise, for the uninitiated), and looking for some ideas that would help them achieve there own objectives more quickly. Now let me throw you something you're not expecting.

Grab a piece of paper and a pen and do the following exercise.

1. **In a single sentence write down the purpose of your new or existing business.**

2. **Now state the date you are expecting it to be a success (in your own terms)**

3. **Now write down when you last had a major strategic brainstorm about your business where you came away buzzing with new ideas and decisions you've made.**

Take no more than sixteen minutes – go!

By the way – are you a passer or player? If you're reading this and have completely passed over doing the above, then I must ask you what's stopping you from actually doing the above? How serious are you about getting the *most* from this book? Maybe as a 'passer', you're also behaving the same way in your business planning? Neglecting the obvious in search of the non-existent?

So may I make a humble request. Go back, get the piece of paper and do the exercise. You'll be glad you did!

Okay. How did you do? A few more questions you can now answer in your head:

1. **How easy did you find the exercise? Give a score out of 10 (10=high).**

2. **How confident you are about achieving success on the date you wrote down? Again, give a score out of 10.**

3. **How much you want your business to succeed – big time? Score out of 10.**

Now before we look at your responses, I want to make an assumption. I am assuming that the business you are in, or the one you are starting, is one that can deliver big exciting returns.

If for example you are setting up a cleaning firm working solely in a hamlet in North Yorkshire and there are eight dwellings only, I am not sure someone is going to come along and write you a cheque for your business at any time in the future.

I am also assuming that you're prepared to think big, bold and brashly, even.

Starting with the scores out of 10, I am hoping that you scored 10, 10 and 10. This would mean that you are on a path of clarity. You've made decisions that you are confidently following through on, and unlike most businesses you actually have a date by which you can confidently tell the world (if you choose to) – my business is a success.

If your scores – any of them are less than 10, let's look at the things you wrote down.

I would define it as *purpose, deadline, passion*.

Every business needs a purpose, deadline and passion around it. If any of these things are missing you must decide right now to rectify it.

Businesses that have a purpose that can't be written down are like a rowing boat without oars. They're adrift with no direction or focus. These businesses can last a while yet inevitably succumb to the next major storm that hits it.

If you have no deadline – no date for success of your business – you've don't have a business; you have a job! Is that what you want? The creation of a job…

Finally let's talk about passion. Look at any really major business success story. I bet you'll find a major slice of passion as part of the building blocks that helped construct its success.

Passion can also be created along the way. Having regular sessions where you work on your business not in your business is a way to inject new success seeds into your venture. And by the way if you're not enjoying your business – what's going on?

So let's now look at **clarity**, keeping decision-making still very much in mind.

Getting clarity and a handle on decision-making

To make good decisions, clarity is where you begin. I have found the most effective tool is a mind map. This is the invention of Tony Buzan, and I would highly recommend you check out Tony Buzan and mind maps on the Internet. Or maybe more specifically on Amazon.com.

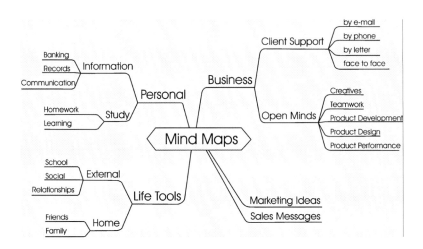

As the name suggests, a mind map is a way of mapping what's in your head on a single sheet of paper. Curious isn't it that if you go to a shop window you are unlikely to look at the contents of the window in a linear fashion, starting at the top left-hand corner and moving across the window – line by line almost, as if reading a book, until you get to the bottom right-hand corner of the display.

This may be how we are taught to read, yet is the most

unnatural way to take in information. If you are like everyone else you will go to a shop window and hop from one part of the display to another as your fancy takes you. You select in a non-linear fashion that information which is of most interest to you at the time. This helps you make up your mind more easily. As you will appreciate, there's a lot of decision-making around shopping. As someone who probably wants to spend as little time in a shop as possible, it certainly supports my outcomes!

So consider using mind maps when you are putting thoughts together or making a valuation of things so far. This will also help you to share your thinking with other people, particularly when you are looking for an informed second or third opinion.

Decision-making is at the heart of every aspect of business and life itself. Despite this, it's curious how we as human beings are rarely taught about effective decision-making. It's one of those subjects that seem to have been left off the school curriculum, yet is a subject which, if mastered, would make a massive difference to all of us. Reviewing my own business, *Results Financial*, it's clear that my current success relates to a number of good decisions made over the years. I've learned that a successful decision-making model must take into account factors like

- **time and timing**

- **money**

- **'unfair' advantages**

- **barriers to success**

- **informed opinions.**

A note of caution, here: if you find yourself adopting a particular decision-making model for all decisions, be aware that there are in fact two types of decision-making that we all face, particularly in business. I refer to big decisions and of course the little ones. There is a case to suggest that all decisions are important in business and making the right little decisions will make it easier for the larger or big decisions to be made more successfully. In my experience, however, I believe that the biggest thing that has daunted me in the past around decision-making, which ultimately has led to things going wrong, is time and timing.

Time and timing

The Spanish have that lovely word 'mañana'. It means tomorrow or at an unspecified future time. In other words it's the Spanish equivalent of procrastination.

In my own industry in the 80s I well remember a piece of legislation which rocked financial advisers across the UK. The Chancellor was to remove LAPR or Life Assurance Premium Relief. At the time, a life assurance policy attracted 15% tax relief. When you think about this, it was truly amazing. For every pound you saved through a life insurance company you got an additional 15p immediately added to your account – that was before any interest was accrued. So, back in 1983, the law changed overnight. I well remember it being a fantastic time for attracting new business, as many people realised it was their last opportunity to open a savings account (for example) that would continue to attract the tax relief. Yet at midnight on a particular day this benefit would be lost forever.

Many insurance company branch offices and other insurance businesses had to decide what steps they were to take. Where I remember it being a bonanza time, it was incredible that a competitor not far from where I worked decided to shut his office down during this period in order to take stock of the situation and assess what impact this new law would have on future business.

It would also be fair to say that the managers of this competitor probably went through no particular decision-making process other than making up their minds using 'ad hoc' methodology. It would also be true to say that I did exactly the same thing; I made a gut decision, probably based largely on my positive frame of mind at the time. Each of us came out with very different outcomes. For me, I had a fantastic business month, whereas I know for a fact my competitor produced very little business during that same timeframe. I suppose what I'm suggesting is that if we had both used the same decision-making model, and if the model worked, we would have probably made the 'right' decision and one that would have produced a positive result for us both.

Time and timing therefore has to be a key decision-making factor. Here in this example time was critical as there was a definite deadline involved. Timing was also a crucial element because there was something momentous happening that would never ever happen again. However, other factors would need to have come into play in order for a good decision to be made by both myself and my competitor.

Opportunity

The next important constituent of any good decision-making model has to be a consideration of 'opportunity'. The question that's always asked of any good entrepreneur is surely "What is the opportunity here that if I turn my back on I would lose forever?" I remember one Christmas going out to buy some presents, when I saw the ideal gift for a member of my family. Given it was Christmas time, which only happens once a year, both time and timing were self-evident. In terms of opportunity, unfortunately a little voice in my head said, "I won't get it today;

I'll pick it up at the weekend when I know I'll be coming back here into town". Needless to say when I returned the item had been sold and the store was unable to re-order any more.

Informed opinion

To really evaluate your opportunity it might be prudent to seek an informed or second opinion from a worthy source. In the example of the Christmas present, it would have been a good move to ask the store concerned how many similar items they had in stock at the time, and also perhaps whether they would be able to re-order the item if the line were to be sold out. What would have been most likely here is that I would have received the strong message that there were only one or two left and that there would be no possibility of re-ordering. This information from an informed source would surely have made me take action immediately.

When obtaining an informed opinion, the source of the opinion will make a big difference. It's important mentally to underline the word 'informed' as any opinion would simply not do. Over the years I've certainly realised that simply obtaining opinions from people can be very confusing, off-putting and indeed be a counter-tool to any decision-making model you use. Therefore when seeking an informed opinion, ensure the source is unbiased and would have some experience in the information being imparted.

'Unfair advantages'

When you've reached a stage of making up your mind based on the last three steps, then the fourth step 'unfair advantages' is a good way to double-check the direction you are currently pointing in. So now make a list of three 'unfair' advantages you personally have in making this decision that others in the same situation do not have. Think about this, as it's something often overlooked.

We are often our own worst enemy. We fail to grasp who we are and what we already have. That little voice in your head is often chattering away incessantly, more often putting you down than building you up.

As a rule of thumb, if you have at least three good reasons why you have an unfair advantage over other people, or one major reason, then the answer in your final decision should be shaping up before your very eyes. If you want to start a music recording business and your favourite cousin, Simon Cowell… I think you get the point.

When I was deciding whether or not to set up *Results Financial*, I had three unfair advantages:

1. **A great deal of experience managing salespeople successfully.**

2. **Capital to fund my venture.**

3. **Quality contacts with people who wanted to bring business to me.**

You will appreciate that the other thing I could have done was to have joined someone else's business as an employee and deferred starting my own business until a later date – but then I would be ignoring the other factors I had previously mentioned.

Barriers to success

Finally, the last factor in my decision-making model is the downside or 'barriers to success'. Here I think of the top three reasons why the decision I'm about to make and the way I am going to make it may be completely wrong, inappropriate or quite simply bad news. You'll find that if you've ticked all the boxes correctly for the previous steps, then it will be somewhat of a chore to think of three good reasons why you should not proceed in the way you're currently thinking. Yet without this rather negative aspect there would be no balance to the process.

Clarifying the model

So here's a decision-making model you might like to use as well:

1. **Time and Timing**

2. **Opportunity**

3. **Informed Opinion**

4. **Unfair advantages**

5. **Barriers to Success**

This five-step model is ideal for big decisions. For smaller decisions like "Shall I buy a new shirt today?" or "Should I take my wife for dinner this evening?" I would use a smaller two-step process:

1. **Time/timing**

2. **Upside/downside**

Here I still ask myself a question around time and timing, as in "If I fail to take action on this occasion, can I come back and made this decision some other time with the same results?" and "Quite simply, what is the upside of deciding 'yes' versus the downside?" I would then weigh up this information in my mind and unless I've got two ticks in my head for the affirmative, I will then proceed with my decision in the negative.

Being able to make good decisions and getting it right almost every time has been a huge benefit to me over the years. I find it extraordinary that so many people starting or running their very own businesses rarely give the idea of having a decision-making process very much thought. I'm very sure there are other decision-making models out there and it might be a good decision for you to explore quite a few of them before you decide which one you would like to use for yourself. What I'm absolutely sure about is the necessity to have something like this and how the lack of it can contribute to the creation of unfortunate and uncalled-for situations and circumstances to get in the way of your future success.

Now if you're still with me, make a decision to come on the rest of this journey. I am eager to take you places where you may not have been before. Ready?

**On the road to success you can be sure of one thing…
there is never a crowd on the extra mile.**

2

Truly Madly Deeply

Passion is a curious word. As we all know, it's most commonly associated with romantic love and relationships. It's also commonly applied to describe feelings about food, wine and cooking, and also to describe feelings about art and artists such as musicians, writers, painters, sculptors and so on.

More and more it's a word used in business, though this usage has only developed over the last twenty or thirty years. Certainly forty years ago few small business owners or managers would ever dare describe having a passion for their products or services.

Even fewer organisations would consider using the word to describe any aspect of customer care. No surprise that in the 50s and 60s it was very much about creating customer satisfaction rather than customer delight. After the Second World War, following years of want and scarcity, the notion of satisfying one's customer was deemed to be wholly adequate and very acceptable. Going the extra mile would have been reasoned as somewhat frivolous and unnecessary.

What's interesting is that we are currently in a phase of business history where lots of organisations talk about passion for their customers, yet very few are actually doing anything serious about it.

I'd like you to imagine passion in the current business thinking context now – something intrinsic and so pivotal in running a small business that I'm sure it will appear very obvious, but despite the fact that the majority of small business entrepreneurs know about its importance, rarely do they consider this powerful success-bringing concept in a way that *really makes the difference to their bottom line.*

Would it surprise you to know that the majority of people who set up a small business do so because they have an idea they'd like to exploit which they also feel would make them money? Probably not. In fact, you may be thinking that this describes your business. Now compare this with a much smaller group of individuals who are completely passionate about why their business is unique and important and know that if they drive this passion in everything they do in and around their business, the money will come automatically. What's ironic is that both groups know in their heart that passion makes all the difference, yet the minority exploit this business gold nugget, and invariably are *always* successful.

It's a bit like sending your children to music lessons because you think they will be more rounded if they can play the piano or violin. This is quite common, and many children go through the motions yet never shine in their musical pursuit, particularly when it's their parents' idea.

At the same time there are children who choose music because it's in their very soul and being and are completely passionate about the results they wish to achieve. Invariably these children are seen as gifted, talented and exceptional. Like Mozart for example. And yes, you may believe he was a genius. I rather fancy it was something a little more fundamental: passion for music in his blood from birth.

I'm going to suggest to you it's about passion in your business first, and skill and knowledge second. Okay, both are important, but there is a distinct priority here as to what must come first. I do know that unless you have a real passion for your small business you will inevitably find what you do tough and unnecessarily challenging.

Before I set up *Results Financial*, I did ask myself the three following pivotal questions:

The Three Passion Checker Questions:

1. **Why would I want to devote the next five to ten years of my life in this new pursuit?**

2. **What do I want to achieve beyond profit and financial considerations?**

3. **How could I ensure that I would remain genuinely motivated behind my quest?**

Apparently, through various surveys, when the owners of small businesses are asked the question, "Why are you in business?" the number one response is, "To make a profit".

Recently Richard Branson announced that all profits from his air and rail businesses would go into environmental projects, including research into a more environmentally-friendly aviation fuel source. Here's a man who understands passion. He's also a wonderful example of an entrepreneur who will always put passion before profit and his outstanding success over the years to me is not surprising when you follow this simple recipe. Once again – when you put passion before profit, profit always finds you in much richer abundance. Think about this for a moment, then compare the premise with your own business or sapling business idea.

As a successful business owner myself, I'm often asked by other entrepreneurs what shaped the success I've attained. I'm always delighted to tell them about passion, yet many look at me if I'm being really boring or cheesy. Few of them however have really embraced the concept and probably all of them believe they are doing it. I always remind myself that when you spell the word belief, at its centre are three letters… **L, I** and **E**. I suppose that's why you should always be careful with what you believe in.

I have no idea who actually coined the phrase: "I love what I do and do what I love." But that's another part of my response, followed by… "and you can too." Curious how I sometimes get a sideways glance that indicates their cynicism.

If you are an entrepreneur – and I suspect you would be if you're still reading this book – I'd like you to write down a score out of 10 for how much passion and love you have in doing what you do. Whether you score low (under 5), or high (between 5 and 9), I'm going to suggest that you have a real challenge that needs a resolution.

I put it to you that as an entrepreneur, unless your score is 10 then you need to sit down and think clearly about what you're devoting your current business life on and, more importantly, why you'd want to pursue something in the future that you are not one hundred percent passionate about.

I remember once sitting at a dinner party discussing the purpose of life, as you do, and one comment has always stuck in my mind ever since. This highly intelligent lady leaned across to me and explained her philosophy. "To me life is like the maze at Hampton Court", she said. "And with any maze there's always a logical and guaranteed systematic way to find the exit. I believe that finding the exit in our very own maze is our life's purpose and what we're missioned with is first to discover the system, then with unbridled passion use the system *until* we find that door of success saying: Well done, here's the exit."

Her comment opened up a whole new world of thinking and inevitable questions. I cited a number of examples where people have followed their dreams and have come completely unstuck. In her opinion, you only come unstuck if you've selected the wrong dream – something you are 9 out of 10 about. She went on to say that life supports anyone who has truly discovered their personal purpose and I smiled when she then listed numerous other examples of well-known people who did just that. These included Florence Nightingale, Winston Churchill, Bill Gates, Richard Branson and Mahatma Ghandi who took on the might of the British Empire single-handed…and won.

The hamburger king

Over the years I have read many books about entrepreneurs with dreams who were passionate about what they wanted to achieve. Another good example is Ray Kroc, the founder of McDonald's restaurants.

Let me ask you to consider what Ray Kroc's passion could have been. Hamburgers? I very much doubt it. Was it perhaps simply about making millions and millions of dollars? Unlikely. Surely it was more about creating a business model so well constructed, that it would work every time.

In fact McDonald's today will probably tell you that they're in the real estate business, not the fast-food business. Their major profits come from selling franchises the world over and leasing the land the restaurants are built on to franchisees.

The story goes that Ray Kroc, at 52 years old, invested his entire life savings to become the exclusive distributor of a milk shake maker called the Multimixer. Hearing about the McDonald's hamburger stand in California owned by Dick & Mac McDonald running eight Multimixers at a time, he packed up his car and headed west. It was 1954. Ray Kroc had never seen so many people served so quickly.

He put forward the idea of opening up several restaurants to the McDonald brothers, convinced that he could sell eight of his Multimixers to each and every one. "Who could we get to open them for us?" Dick McDonald said. "Well," Kroc answered, "What about me?"

41

Ray Kroc opened the Des Plaines, Illinois restaurant in 1955 and never looked back. Today, there are tens of thousands of McDonald's restaurants serving millions of people daily around the world. The incredible growth and success of McDonald's can be summed up with the first thought that went through Ray Kroc's mind when he first saw McDonald's: "This will go any place."

In fact it was the system they were deploying that most took Ray Kroc's attention and it was the system that he ultimately purchased from them as opposed to the recipe for the hamburgers, for example. It was also the system that ultimately was so good that it brought in vast amounts of business, not by single customers to his restaurant but entrepreneurs who wanted to reproduce his restaurant in their part of the country.

It's my understanding that what emerged as Ray Kroc's passion was his falling in love with the idea of the system that happened to create hamburgers in the most effective and profitable manner.

By continuing to work to improve this system, he ended up making one giant of a business that became the most successful hamburger business in history. In fact in the early days he would revoke those franchisees who refused to follow his system one hundred percent.

Part of the contract they signed was that they would stick rigidly to the system without fail. The moment they introduced their own ideas or made changes to the way the system worked, he had every right to refund their franchise fee and take the franchise back. This was the extent of his passion around an idea that became the fabric of his very being.

You don't have to be a Ray Kroc to have passion in what you do. My passion is about making it easy for financial advisers to offer the most comprehensive and professional advice available to customers along with integrity and the highest levels of customer care.

Since starting *Results Financial*, I've not met any similar UK entrepreneur who is growing a business with the same passion. On a month by month basis I am constantly reviewing our systems and the ways we work to ensure we're doing things to the best of our ability. This is undeniably a strong passion that drives me and in turn supports and motivates the team that go to make up who we are and how we do what we do so well. I'm not out of the maze yet, but know in my heart the exit that relates to my business purpose as opposed to my entire life's purpose is tantalisingly close. Finding the exit requires an 'Exit Strategy', and when I can see the door telling me this is the way out, I know it will simply make finding the ultimate exit door in life infinitely easier.

I was explaining this concept to a business associate recently, and he got completely the wrong end of the stick. Life's exit isn't death! It is about realising what your life is truly about, and achieving a level of success…that if you were to pass away at that moment, you'd have absolutely no regrets whatsoever. That sounds like heaven to me.

The passion challenge

It's not always easy to add the passion component to what you do if it's not already there. If there's a simple way of dealing with this, and you're in total agreement that being 10 out of 10 in terms of passion is important, then here are some more suggestions for moving forward:

1. **Remind yourself what it was (apart from profit) that made you decide to embark on the business you're currently running.**

2. **If you did choose your business purely for profit, what could you get truly passionate about that would make the whole venture more exciting and ultimately infinitely more rewarding?**

3. **Define what element of the business is the most important and interesting to you. By doing this and being more passionate about that one aspect, could you perhaps delegate other elements of the business to other individuals who are more passionate than you about these other areas?**

4. **Re-evaluate your business and ask the question – is there any other type of business you could be more passionate about? In other words are you in the right business in the first place?**

The challenge with number 4 is that if you decide you're in the wrong business it may not be financially viable to extricate yourself. This is a tough one and invariably the dilemma is whether to soldier on or cut your losses. If you're in this situation, it will be important to get a second opinion from as many sources as possible before you ultimately decide what you should do. I suppose it's a bit like a marriage that's not working. Do you soldier on and cross your fingers or do you have a serious conversation, and assuming things can't be put right, part company and both rediscover true passion that's painfully missing from the current situation?

I think you probably know what I would choose in the last example, because passion in what you do is so very important and once you've clarified what your passion is and really experience its immense feeling of fulfilment, even though you've not got the final result yet, being in this strong position offers you the most immensely rewarding feeling of heading in the right direction, and being ready to take on the world.

44

I can't change the direction of the wind, but I can adjust my sails to always reach my destination.

Jimmy Dean

3

The 'Gerber' Factor

A book that really woke me up ten years ago was *The E-Myth* by Michael Gerber. Today this is a relatively well-known account of how to run a successful business. Though not all of it would be appropriate for every business, a great deal of the content of this good read does make you think and can help you to stay on the right path in terms of starting and successfully running a small to medium-sized enterprise.

Apart from recommending this book, or its successor, *The E-Myth Revisited*, I'd like to share with you what's really worked for me and I really believe it would help anyone keen enough to ensure their business is built on a firm footing. Earlier I mentioned how many business owners are unclear as to what exactly the purpose of their business is. Apart from the most popular comment "Making a profit" or "Being successful", there are also those who simply want to be their own boss and just ensure the mortgage is paid. That's like owning a swimming pool and only ever sitting on the side for a quick paddle. For me Gerber provided the high diving board with instructions how to use it.

When I originally read the book and understood the message that Gerber was offering, that the purpose of a business is to sell it, a bright light bulb went on in my head. People get confused when they read anything about selling their business, because often the reaction is "but why would I want to sell it?". You could say the same thing about buying a house. You buy it to live in it and enjoy it. Nothing wrong with that. Yet, if you were to buy a house and think that the purpose of being there was to sell it as quickly as possible for the highest possible amount, surely the house would end up being in immaculate shape fast and extremely desirable not only for a potential buyer but for you, the inhabitant. Which house would you prefer to live in? One that was just habitable or one that was luxurious, very comfortable and a joy to go home to?

Similarly with a business, if you build a business from the start with a view to selling it, even though you may never do this, then boy will you be running an amazing enterprise! And that's Gerber's point. Out there in the world there are a number of big corporations that are built on this principle and McDonald's restaurants, as described above, is one good example of this. Here you have a business where everything within it has been thought out to maximum effectiveness and profit advantage. As the product is not the hamburger, but the business itself, it shifts the focus for the owner in terms of what they put their energy into.

Setting aside McDonald's for a moment, I remember reading this and then thinking about the business I was about to set up. At the end of this chapter you may like to see an article I wrote in an industry magazine which for months on end attracted the most amazing volume of enquiries, letters and positive messages.

So think about this. If you were to liken building a business in the same way you built a house for a moment. With a house you'd start with the foundations, then the walls and roof, making sure the interior was as it should be. Many people build their businesses by starting with maybe some walls, then the roof on, only to realise that some foundations needed to go in which is now going to be very difficult with the walls and roof in place. No wonder their building of their business is constantly in a state of flux, never properly finished or constantly in a state of disrepair or constant poorly orchestrated refurbishment.

For me 'Gerber's Gold' covered the following concepts:

1. **What's the purpose of the business? In order to achieve this goal, what exactly do you want to create in order to sell it?**

2. **Who are you going to have in your business from day one? What would be their role? Will you have all the bases covered for what's required?**

3. **Will you have identified all of the processes required to run the business? Who would be responsible for putting the processes together? Who will check that the processes are working effectively?**

4. **How will you differentiate yourself in the marketplace? What makes you different from the competition?**

With *Results Financial* it was important for me to answer all these questions before launching the business and there's no surprise, perhaps, that I've been complimented many times over on running a very organised business with very little paperwork for a financial services organisation. If you were to visit our premises, you'd notice clarity, space, tidiness and lots of sleek business processes. I like to think about the business as a well-lubricated old-fashioned Swiss watch. Wheels within wheels that move with precision that can't help but produce ideal results.

In a business like ours we need to have this high-quality style business with robust systems in place, given that we are helping people to invest and organise their assets and investments which invariably mean everything to them. For us to be disorganised in any way would lose the confidence of our clients and the success we've built up over the years. This also surely applies to the running of any business. If customers knew you were running a business that had no foundation it's unlikely they'd spend any money with you. Sadly we all know too well that such businesses do come and go and sometimes they go in the middle of transactions with customers. The result is chaos and bad feelings, particularly when customers lose money as a result.

Primary aim

Alongside Gerber's thoughts I also remember thinking about my primary aim. Here's something that few business owners ever contemplate or perhaps dare to contemplate. Let me ask you for a moment,

What's your primary aim in life?

Before you answer, unless you've already thought this through properly the chances are that any swift response is likely to be mere conjecture rather than what is in fact true.

It's extraordinary how most humans are wandering generalities rather than 'meaningful specifics'. In other words they are meandering in their lives rather than knowing precisely who they are, what they're here to do and how they intend to achieve it.

Thinking on these lines is often sobering stuff, and yet knowing your primary aim and linking it to why, what and how you run your business is immensely inspirational. Though I've never had the pleasure of meeting Richard Branson, I rather suspect he's really thought through his primary aim and life's purpose, and its link to his successful business enterprises has made a big difference to his overall success in life. After all, there have been other airline entrepreneurs who have come and gone because their primary motivation was mainly financial with little else in mind.

I've certainly noticed time and time again that my success has come from clarity about why I set up my business in the first place, what it would involve and how it would operate. I've also regularly channelled my thoughts with mental reminders on a daily basis of what I've wanted to achieve year by year. I'm delighted to say that what I'd foreseen has largely come to pass and what is left to still happen is now infinitely more likely than ever before.

Where primary aim is concerned, the best approach is one that encapsulates both business goals and your life's higher purpose. This makes things very easy to grasp and deal with. I do appreciate however that for some people their primary aim for life is very different to their business primary aim. My concern would be a mismatch between these two aims and the possibility of confusion that arises from having more than one defined direction.

Returning to Gerber, another light bulb moment for me was really understanding that to run a successful business, I'd have to be able to create the option that at any time I could step away from it and the business would run itself without me being there. Though that initially felt like a dream that I was pursuing, over the years that's exactly what has happened. Today I'm able to take many holidays and breaks from the business and return without losing anything. In fact some of my team think that the business runs even more effectively and profitably when I'm not there! If you can say the same thing about your business – that it runs successfully whether you're there or not – then I firmly believe you've achieved something that few small businesses are ever able to achieve.

In addition to this, you should ideally have created a profitable business that could be sold to a third party, enabling the third party to reap the same rewards as you are currently enjoying. There are many, many chequebooks open the world over with people eager to buy profitable enterprises. For many of them, they're not at all concerned with the industry as long as the process is profitable and stable. Some people renovate houses; others renovate businesses. If the truth be known, anyone can build a successful business. You simply need to get the foundations right and solid systems in place from the earliest opportunity. So take a look at this article that was first published in the LIA magazine.

Five moves...
to a more successful business

There was a time when Michael Bell didn't look forward to going into the office, principally because he was just 'doing a job' rather than creating a huge opportunity. Today, things are different. Something radical has happened, and if he's office bound, he can't wait to get there.

You're probably intrigued to know what happened to make such a huge difference to my life in financial services; it was, in fact, a small combination of things. Five simple things that anyone can do, but few put into practice.

It started with a huge brainstorm session. I decided to spend the day with someone very special. Myself! I'd picked this idea up at an LIA talk some time back but today was the day I decided to actually put the idea into practice. Was I in for a surprise. The ideas simply flowed on to my empty page. I began to evaluate what I wanted from my business, who I wanted as clients, how I was going to offer added value to the chosen few and how to get into high net worth and corporate financial planning. At the end of the day, I had, for the first time in my financial career, a clear-cut path laid out in simple steps. So far, so good.

At the time I was working on my own. However I wanted to build a team of advisers, but clearly wanted to make my business fly so that I could attract the right type of individual. I wanted to work with like-minded individuals – those with an entrepreneurial spirit not a 'working to make a living' mentality.

Next, I discovered systems and their power. If you want to see systems at work, be a customer in any McDonald's restaurant. The system sells hamburgers very effectively. Of course I was selling something more sophisticated, but until that point I'd never thought 'system'. Rather, I'd make up the system on the spot and invariably it would be different. I also discovered myself and what I was capable of.

This came from some serious exploration of personal effectiveness. I began to read widely, bought some tapes and videos and even got myself a coach.

Yet, a major key was still to be implemented: My product and service. This is what foxed me to begin with because I assumed, as many people do, that life assurance was a main product line, and my service was selling it to those who most needed it.

Needed a coat hanger

The stark reality was that nothing could be further from the truth. I had yet to invent my product; my coat hanger if you like, that the suit called 'financial planning' could hang upon. The moment I presented such a system to the unsuspecting world of prospects... I got the most warm and positive reaction. Yes, they bought financial services, lots of it, but they were only doing so because of the coat hanger. For the first time they could see how it all linked together and how it was true financial planning, not me simply selling cold unconnected plans and policies.

What's your coat hanger? What differentiates you from everyone else?

*I also desperately needed a 'marketing engine'; my way of systematising my prospecting. An engine runs on pistons. I was going to have four of these to start with and feature a new one... the corporate market. Apparently there are 3.6 million SMEs (small to medium-sized businesses) in the UK who do not have any professional financial planning – according to the DTI. The question: How do I tap into this market? I use an unusual mailshot approach, which works for me. But it was more about doing **something**, rather than what most people do which is **nothing**. Action is the key.*

Yes, they bought financial services, lots of it, but they were only doing so because of the coat hanger.

Golden rules

In summary, I suppose I can put my business success and the pleasure I derive from it down to these golden rules:

1. *Know what you want in detail.*
2. *Create systems to support your objectives.*
3. *Have a truly unique product.*
4. *Ensure your service is also different.*
5. *Create a marketing engine that works for you and never let it seize up!*

(LIA Prospect Magazine, May 2000)

**Tentative efforts lead to tentative outcomes.
Therefore give yourself fully to your endeavours.
Decide to construct your character through excellent
actions and determine to pay the price of a
worthwhile goal. The trials you encounter will
introduce you to your strengths. Remain steadfast ...
and one day you will build something that endures.
Something worthy of your potential.**

Ipectetus, Roman teacher and philosopher 55-135 AD

4

People Are Your Lifeblood

A few decades ago, most businesses treated the people in an organisation as a mere resource. Today, 'Human Resources' as a term is gradually being phased out. The new buzz word is 'talent', and not before time. It's for this reason that I've never favoured the word 'staff' in a business and always preferred 'people', 'colleagues' or, better still, 'team'.

There's no question that the people in any business make the business. They are the MAD factor – where MAD stands for 'Make A Difference'. People in the business affect your brand, business image, what your customers think about you and whether you enjoy going into work every day. You can have the smartest offices in the best part of town in an industry that's fun to be in, and yet if the people in your organisation are not up to scratch, the outcomes heading your way are normally disastrous.

Here in the UK, having employees is a big responsibility. If you employ someone it's not a simple matter of getting rid of them if things aren't working out. So the interview is a crucial component in attracting the right people. What exacerbates the situation today is the importance also of being politically correct – not discriminating around gender, background, age and so on. This is as it should be, yet I'm always amused when reminded that the words 'enthusiastic' and 'energetic' could be construed as being prejudicial in an advertisement for new people. In my organisation I'm definitely looking for energetic and enthusiastic team members regardless of their gender, background or age and I can't imagine employing somebody who is dull, de-energised and has no enthusiasm for their role.

At *Results Financial* we have a great team. I rarely have any people issues and often get positive comments from suppliers, visitors and, of course, clients. There are a few tools and tips that I have used on occasions that have made a significant difference but I'm fully aware that how I run the people side of my business isn't the normal modus operandi for most businesses.

No secrets

If any member of my team asks me for the sales figures for the month, our outgoings or tax position, I have no hesitation in supplying the information. In fact where figures are concerned, I like to be transparent and open. Ten years ago there was a new revolution called 'Open Book Management' where companies were urged by business gurus to be completely 'upfront' and 'on the table' about financial matters in the business. I have to agree that this approach is a good one. When members of the team know how expensive stationery is for example, and what sort of impact this outgoing has on the bottom line, they're more likely to be wary of wasting this valuable resource and happy to make suggestions when supplies can be purchased more cheaply elsewhere. It is also true for companies that where they have lean months, if the people in the organisation are aware of the fact they are more likely to work more effectively and do things that help address the situation, even on some occasions find new business streams.

Proper communication

If your business consists of four or more people, then it becomes quite important to ensure everyone knows what's happening. If you're working in an organisation that's slow or lax in keeping the team informed, then this can lead to communication breakdown, misunderstandings and a lack of unity.

The way it was once explained to me is as follows. Imagine a metal bar, non-magnetised compared with one that is. One has a power that is near enough visible and the other one appears to have no power at all. If you also imagine that within the bars are little forces like arrows, the non-magnetised bar's arrows are probably facing in every possible direction where the forces or arrows in the magnetised bar are all pointing in the same direction.

If we take this analogy a step further and suggest that these are two different businesses of the same size, one is a stagnant enterprise while the other is a directed focused organisation. I've always thought it's the job of any good leader of an organisation to bear this in mind when recruiting, communicating and being transparent. If you're operating an organisation which is focused and directed then the business has a movement or momentum all of its own and the decisions you make as a leader would ideally need to fall in line with keeping this movement or momentum going.

The classic 360° feedback

The other thing you may like to think about is putting your neck on the block and allowing as many people from your organisation as possible to offer you some 'soul food', both good and challenging if need be, for you to ensure you too are pointing in the right direction. This is a tough one because ideally you need to ask not only people in your organisation but also those outside, including most importantly your clients. A bit like a client advisory board to check how the company is doing, this one would be set up for you and you alone as leader of the organisation. If you are a team leader, this is still a very useful exercise. Naturally, once you have all the information to hand, it's important to take on board what needs to change and then decide how you intend to change it.

Pushing the boat out

I know there are some businesses that go completely overboard in terms of socialising after working hours. They have clubs, societies and a whole myriad of events during the year in an attempt to keep people happy and working well as a team. This can be overdone. Work/life balance does mean a respect for people's families and the fact that they need quality time at home as well as the workplace.

I take great pleasure in occasionally inviting people to my home. My team often see this as a great privilege, where I see it as an equal privilege for me that they accept the invitation. Either way, this does bring people together and it gives me an opportunity to meet people's other halves. You can tell a lot by the person they've married or have opted to share their life with. I particularly like to do this little exercise before taking someone new on board. One of the last things I suggest before a final decision on my part is to meet their other half.

People tools

There are a couple of people tools I would recommend to any business. I'm not suggesting these should definitely be used as it very much depends on outcome requirements. They're tools I've used now and then to great effect.

1. The short burst meeting

The short burst meeting can be anything from one minute to five. It should be done standing up and with as much adrenalin as possible. Good times for the short burst meeting would be first thing in the morning, during the middle of the day or at the end of the day. It's a kind of round-up of ideas and at the same time a way to get people all on the same boat, on the same river and in the same water current. It's good to have different people orchestrate and lead this mini meeting of minds and you may like to try them regularly for a while to see the impact they will inevitably have. A possible downside is that the meetings go on longer (sometimes infinitely longer) than planned so I strongly urge you to have someone as timekeeper to ensure this doesn't happen. Even a 60-second meeting can pack a mighty punch if it's well organised. Such a meeting allows you to understand what everyone else is doing today and your part in it. To have another one of these at the end of the day can tie things up rather well. The more communication going on within a team the better and the sad reality is that the opposite is more likely to be true in many UK businesses.

2. The traffic lights

I have it on good authority that people rarely make up their mind on the spot. The majority of humans like to hear about something, think about it, then think about it one more time before making a decision. Using the 'traffic light system' is a good way to tap into this psychology whilst making it easier and fairer when something new is being introduced or a change is about to happen.

The traffic light system, as it indicates, revolves around red, amber and green. When you want to introduce a new idea, you send out a red communication normally by email, to all members of the team. This outlines what the proposals are for the change and will encourage comments, thoughts and contributions in terms of a reaction to the proposal. The amber communication will go out soon after to incorporate the comments and suggestions that have been received and people will realise that unless they speak up now, a final, green communication will be despatched cementing the change as permanent. This three-step process allows team input around any change in the business. People like to have their say and sometimes what they say is so useful it really does make a noticeable difference to the final result.

When things go wrong

Disciplinary issues can be very demoralising for all concerned. Some companies have absolutely no idea how to conduct these and if the wrong approach takes place it can become a scar that will be difficult to heal. The key to any potentially unpleasant conversation has to be a positive mindset from the start. When entering the dangerous waters around being critical about another person, the starting place must be an appreciation of what's good about them rather than what's bad. This appears so obvious and yet is completely overlooked when things have gone wrong with a member of the team.

Of course there will be situations when an individual has completely messed up in one way or another and it's possible that they've been unreliable, dishonest or lacked integrity. The fact is that if they're going to continue to be a member of the organisation they need to feel that there's a second chance for them, otherwise you have one of your arrows pointing in completely the opposite direction to all the others.

When a City broker firm lost £5 million in a single transaction based on a mistake of one of the traders, the managing director was asked if he was going to sack the individual involved. "Not when it's just cost me £5 million to train them," was his comment. I suppose it really all does depend on how you view things.

The people in any business are the lifeblood of the organisation. Without them there is no blood flow and you are left with an empty shell. Treat your team with respect and they will invariably respect you. Catch people doing things right before anything else and always have time to listen and reflect when a member of your business needs to communicate their concerns. Your team are an investment. And like any good investment, they will become more valuable with time.

**Enthusiasm is like a ripple on the water.
It spreads.**

5

The Power of Mindset

When I first joined the financial services industry I remember that a lot of emphasis was placed on attitude and behaviour, seemingly before contemplating business strategy. I think it fair to say that of all the industries in the world, financial services is the number one for getting attitude, behaviour and thinking right before anything else. At least it used to be. Having said this, I have noticed over recent times that this important part of the industry's culture is being eroded by a new wave of traditional thinking which places less emphasis on attitude and behaviour and more emphasis on statistics, analysis and business protocol. So I was pleased to have come in when I did. The mindset focus made a huge impact on my stepping up to the plate, then taking the plunge off the high diving board. I learned from some of the most successful financial advisers on the planet that without the right mindset you can end up being a very successful failure.

Just to expand on this a little more, it's a well-known fact that some of the most successful people in the world are not necessarily the most qualified. In fact the most qualified individuals, many of whom have business qualifications and a string of letters after their name, are great on the theory and pretty poor on putting it into action. "Is this because you don't have any qualifications?" I hear you asking. Well I am, of course, very qualified for my professional position though I don't have a university degree. Of course in an ideal world it would be great to be highly qualified and highly successful. I'm quite happy with just the latter at the moment. The point that many miss is that you can be outrageously successful without being highly qualified; and yes there are always exceptions. Having the right behaviour and attitude as a surgeon won't get you very far if you have no medical qualifications! So my broad concept thinking mainly applies to the business world and the entrepreneur, and on this level I am steadfast in my beliefs.

It's very much my goal here to give you enough support, information, tools and techniques for you to make a significant difference to either your existing business or the new one you're about to set up. Right now in the first decade of the new century, there's never been a better opportunity for individuals to be extremely successful in running their own businesses. With the advent of the Internet, marketing has become easier and a much more effective process for those who are brave enough to grasp some of the basics.

Over the years I've discovered and realised that one of the fundamental factors for success is being able to get up every morning with the right attitude between my ears. A positive and proactive approach to life and business leads to the right behaviours and actions alongside making the right decisions and ultimately attaining great results. Yet all of this is underpinned by one factor which is often ignored. I refer to beliefs.

What I find quite extraordinary is how most people believe that the little voice in their head, which (as I have mentioned earlier and will mention again) is continually chattering away, tells the truth one hundred percent of the time. The reality is, that depending on your mindset, some of us are plagued with waves of negative thinking through incorrect assumptions and beliefs that we're allowing to permeate our subconscious on a regular basis.

Those of us who are aware of this trap and have done something about it have improved the situation by getting into the habit of thinking positively far more often than allowing negativity to take control. It sounds a little cheesy, though dare I say very true, that *you have to believe to achieve.* Historically success has rested in the laps of those who have gone out to achieve it with the belief that they would be able to. The reverse of this is also painfully true.

In setting up my own business I remember having at least a couple of conversations with people who would, as friends, warn me of the pitfalls of setting up my own business and remind me that running a business is complex, difficult and would expose me to the possibility of financial disaster. Although these individuals were well-meaning, had I taken their so-called good advice I would certainly not be writing this book or enjoying all the fruits of my positive labours.

The 'Faking It' factor

Channel 4 television's *Faking It* series was a revelation to me. To take someone from one occupation and with careful coaching by those who knew what they were doing, train the individual in something completely different in thirty days, was great to witness. I remember a wonderful episode where a bicycle courier became a polo player in a month, without any equestrian background or the faintest understanding of the game. Incidentally, in the final exercise where judges were asked to spot the 'fake' player, he wasn't chosen at all.

In early financial services, people came from every imaginable profession and occupation to sell insurance and related products. There were teachers, police officers, home makers, ex company directors and even funeral directors. They all, in a very short space of time, learned about family protection and were sent out to sell company products in the blink of an eye. Okay, not a good state of affairs I grant you – hence the Financial Services Act 1986. There were many successes as there were failures, though it's one concept I'd ask you to consider for a moment.

Imagine if you could be coached in a very short space of time to be successful in, for example, running your very own business regardless of the industry or discipline. Or, in the context of your existing job, think about the difference three 'new' skills would make to your current success if you could summon them from the potential you already possess. After all, the polo player was of course always a polo player deep inside, wasn't he? It simply took someone to come along with the right tools to 'tease' the ability out.

This thinking means that, right now, you're probably infinitely more powerful and successful than you'd ever give yourself credit for, and herein lies the challenge. There's one thing that's stopping you achieving whatever you want in your life, and that thing I call *interference*.

I was first introduced to interference by my business coach, Glen McCoy many years ago. It was one of those realisations that made instant sense. The idea that all of us have a voice on our shoulder, in our heads or glued to our left ear that constantly chatters away to us about, well – everything. This is the chattering voice I have referred to earlier. It's judge, jury and executioner all rolled into one. It filters ideas and ensures anything we think about or consider matches our core beliefs. If there's a strong match we accept the thought and if there isn't we reject it.

The voice has two faces, a positive and negative. Sadly, with most of us, it's the negative side that controls us, creating a great deal of self-limitation. The question I originally asked myself was… how understanding this fundamental truth could positively affect my future. Then, of course, it dawned on me. If there was a way of controlling the negative voice, or even better, re-programming it, imagine what I could set myself up to do, be and have!

There's no question that the success of my current business *Results Financial* was as a direct outcome of setting my interference aside nine years ago. The financial services industry was in a major transition phase, No one wanted to speculate about its future. The old guard of financial advisers were deserting the industry en masse, and new legislation seemed to be coming at practitioners from every direction.

Of course there was also plenty of external interference that I had to deal with – friends (at least that was what they called themselves), who told me why my plans were short-sighted and why I was wasting my time, not to mention those who guaranteed that I would fail.

The magic in dealing with interference comes with one simple philosophy. When you've worked out ten ways of why you'll never succeed, think about three ways in which you could, then choose one of these ideas and pursue it for thirty days regardless, then reassess the situation. It's about spending your energy and focus on what you can achieve, not what you can't.

In looking at those in my life who've supported and inspired me, I'm clear that there's an unerring law, and I'm going to call it *The Faking It Factor*. Quite simply, if you're able to set aside the little voice and have sufficient desire to get your desired outcome, then after thirty brief days of application, an exciting result will unfold.

The question, "How do you get rid of the negative voice?" is what I'd like to tackle next. If it was as straightforward and easy to achieve, then everyone would be doing it.

Now I don't want to be that voice right now telling you it's not an easy thing to achieve. I will tell you however that though it does need some effort, it's ultimately highly achievable and in essence very simple. The other good news is that the more you quieten the negative voice, the less effort it takes to keep in check, and your thinking takes on a new style that focuses more on what is possible than what is not.

Over the years I've attended many motivational events, presentations, talks, workshops and read endless books related to positive thinking. What jumps out at me now is the complete realisation that there is no value in the expression 'think positive'. That's a bit like saying, 'be rich'. What does 'think positive' really entail? How do you know if you are doing it properly? When do you get an outcome by doing this?

If we go back to *Faking It* for a moment, in this great series, there were those who fell by the wayside also – for example, the Yorkshire lass who was sent to London to become a debutante. In this particular episode, despite going through the process, she was easily spotted at the end, and I sat there thinking why on earth did she volunteer for this in the first place? Throughout the exercise she appeared to be fighting her potential transformation, and did not have the desire to make it work. Positive thinking, then, isn't something you can be given, or suddenly take on board by reading a book on the subject. A critical element has to be desire, and not any old desire, but something you are passionate about. There's that word again.

I did say this can be a challenge for some people. Passion and desire is a natural feeling that the human race needs to survive, which is why it's something already inside us. Imagine how we would be doing as a civilisation if we had to force ourselves to want to procreate as if it were an effort-laden chore. We'd have surely died out centuries ago…

The mind – a place to start

I remember being shown 'The Iceberg Principle' some time back. Imagine your mind is a giant iceberg and as such the majority of it is out of sight in the sea with a small tip in view. Most of us concentrate on the bit that we're aware of, and we completely ignore the potential that's out of our sight called the subconscious. If we're able to influence our subconscious, the part we're largely unaware of, our beliefs change which affects our behaviours and our ultimate results.

One of the simplest ways of achieving this is through the use of MindChangers. My coach introduced me to the concept over ten years ago. I took his advice and used these awesome tools on a regular daily basis. Over the years the results I achieved, I firmly believe, could be largely attributed to having my mind in the right gear and focused on the right things in the right direction. This, if nothing else, is one major advantage of regular MindChangers. Though there are various MindChanger techniques, I am going to share one with you which, if you do regularly, will make a big impact on your business, and overall success.

MindChanger cards

Go to a stationers and buy yourself a pack of lined record cards. Ideally you should buy a pack which has different colours. You may then wish to attribute a colour to an area of your life you want to improve. The instructions are very simple:

1. **On each card write a separate goal or objective.**

2. **Have a total of no more than thirty cards.**

3. **Have a minimum of twenty cards.**

4. **Read the cards at least once a day, or more often if you wish.**

5. **Save the card when it's achieved and write the date of achievement on it.**

6. **Replace achieved cards with new goals and objectives.**

7. **Keep the cards secret and do not share them with anyone, other than perhaps your life partner. The reason for this is that in sharing your goals and ambitions with others you may also attract negative comments and unwanted interference.**

In a nutshell, on a daily basis I read my thirty cards which must take me three or four minutes maximum. Each card has a separate goal that I'm looking to achieve and very often I'll have several cards with the same subject, written in a different way. Now here's the magic. Each card is worded as if the goal or objective has already been achieved. For example, if your goal is to run a very successful business, having a card which simply says '*I will run a very successful business*' is probably going to do little to engage your subconscious. However, if you write '*Isn't it amazing how successful my business has been? I'm over the moon!*' your subconscious mind is initially going to be confused. It will be thinking 'but I haven't even started my new business yet'. Of course, this is the point.

When you make a statement to your subconscious as if it's already happened, the only way your subconscious can deal with it eventually is to assume it to be true. Then it will open every 'mental window' to allow the goal to materialise. It's not magic, just the engaging of the RAS or Reticular Activation System in your brain. For example, try driving your car and see how many white vehicles are on the road today. I promise you, you'll be stunned. Hundreds of them. But where were they yesterday? Well, they were still on the roads, only your mental window file called 'white car' was closed. Being successful is often pinned on opening enough mental windows to support what you want. Sounds complex, yet it's so very simple.

People often ask me why you need as many as twenty cards.

I liken it to going to the gym. If you were asked to do some press-ups, would you do two or three or at least twenty? The fact is, the mind is like a muscle in your body. It needs some consistency of exercise before it shapes up. So yes, twenty cards minimum, thirty maximum. Also, like exercise, you can overdo it and this can have the reverse effect, which is why there is a maximum.

I've always been surprised at how simple this technique is and how dramatically successful it has been over the years for me. Cynics often say it has very little to do with the technique and more about myself, and as much as this is a wonderful compliment, I know that those members of my team who have adopted this very same mindset tool have had their own measure of personal success. Guess what: the more you do the technique, the more successful you'll get.

As an entrepreneur, your mindset and the way you think about your business will undoubtedly dictate the outcomes further down the line. It's like the classic story of the shoe salesman who went to an African country back in the 60s and came back on the next flight reporting that there was no demand for shoes in this area of Africa as no one wore them. His successor flew out the following week and ended up setting up a successful business after his excited report back to his company that this was exactly the place they needed to be as the market for shoes was massive.

In my own industry, people have been reluctant to join because of their perception that no one out there wants financial services and certainly the sale of life assurance is largely a waste of time. I joined the industry with completely the opposite idea. I knew that if life assurance was free, everyone would want it in vast quantities. There's no question that it is an amazing and important product and the challenge of being successful in the industry is convincing potential clients of the facts of life... and death. Properly communicated in a professional manner with integrity, this inevitably leads me to making a sale where everyone is delighted with the outcome.

The other ways I've managed to grow and develop a powerful mindset is to read books, listen to CDs and watch movies which are in some way inspirational. One of my favourite movies of all time in this genre is *Dead Poets Society*. This delightful tale, starring Robin Williams, is very much worth watching, though it was made a good twenty years ago. My suggestion is to watch it the first time for enjoyment and then watch it a second time with a large notepad and pencil and write down the myriad phrases, ideas and inspirational concepts that are tucked neatly in the script.

Once a year I also like to visit the *Million Dollar Round Table* which is a worldwide professional body for my industry. Invariably the event is in the USA and fellow colleagues come together for a week of presentations, discussions, seminars, conferences and workshops. Some of the speakers are so inspirational that it is not unusual to go back to your office the following week and produce some stunning results on your newly recharged batteries. I sometimes get asked by people why on earth I'd want to travel all that way to listen to things that I've probably heard many times before. Quite simply, all of us need support and encouragement throughout our lives. It starts at school and is a never-ending requirement. If the messages are positive and consistent, we tend to have a quality behaviour and attitude process installed in our minds that help us deliver outstanding results.

Two things I will never forget...

When I first became self employed, my sales manager took me to lunch and shared these two gems with me:

1. **Live each day in time compartments. Do not think about yesterday or worry about tomorrow. Yesterday is spent, tomorrow is a promissory note, but today is cash. The only time to look back is if you want to go in that direction.**

2. **Rid yourself of 'drain people', i.e. people who drain away your energy by means of their attitude. Do not drive yourself crazy trying to figure our why they act the way they do. Liars are supposed to lie, cheaters are supposed to cheat and complainers are supposed to complain! Unless you are intending to open a rehabilitation clinic, rid yourself of 'drain people'.**

If you're one of those individuals who needs some inspiration and help, I will be more than delighted to send you a list of inspired learning, listening and reading. Email me personally at mbell@resultsfinancial.co.uk. Here's to your great future!

Success is a journey, not a destination. The doing is often more important than the outcome.

Arthur Ashe

6

Attracting New Business

One of the most challenging areas of any business is how to get the business to come through the door. If it's a shop you run how do you attract the footfall of new customers? If it's an Internet business, how do you get the volume of people visiting your site? And if you're in financial services, how do you get new clients queuing outside the office?

There must be over a hundred solid ideas around attracting new business and I'd like to share the best ideas that have worked at *Results Financial*.

1. Personal introductions

Certainly the best way I've ever done business is by personal introductions. Some people call them referrals or recommendations and I like to think that anything less than a personal introduction is going to be of low quality. In order to get personal introductions you have to do one very simple thing – *ask for them*. This is the bit that daunts most people. Their paradigm is that clients and customers are going to be more than unhappy when quizzed about who they may know. Nothing could be further from the truth. The classic advice I recall from childhood was always, "If you don't ask, you don't get." This has always been a truism for me.

When I first became a salesman in full-time selling, I always felt a little bashful in asking the question. I was to discover that some clients were feeling the same way about asking me whether I would mind helping members of their family and friends! It got to the point where I realised that the worst that could happen is for someone to politely say "no". The best that could happen is you get given more business to build the foundation of your organisation. I soon realised that not asking was pure lunacy and asking equated to a good professional business practice that in the main was welcomed.

The best way of going about this is to drop a hint early on that you make it a professional business practice to work by personal introductions and I promise you that it immediately occurs to the customer or client that you are going to ask them at some future point. When you do, there's no surprise. Simple. And by the way, immensely rewarding.

2. Networking

My second favoured method is networking. I just love this idea, be it at a party, social event or business meeting. Exchanging business cards and simultaneously exchanging business backgrounds can be a fascinating experience. The key to really good networking is finding ways of linking your contacts with their contacts. I appreciate that this advice may appear somewhat obvious, but people often fail to do the obvious.

In my experience, when you do offer a connection other people feel obliged to do exactly the same for you. In my business sector networking has produced thousands and thousands of pounds of business over the years. With the advent of websites, I like to take someone's business card, look at their website address, reflect and then suggest to them that I ring them after I've had a look at it. I'm sure you'll appreciate that more times than not people like the thought of some feedback about their site and welcome the chance to speak to you subsequently. The key is to have a reason to ring them after you've taken their card. If you articulate the reason with their card in your hand you anchor the moment in their memory and when you ring them at a future occasion they were half expecting your call.

I recall one financial services colleague who, in the late 70s, decided to only accept high-quality and financially independent clients. He ended up travelling first class on a cruise liner where he knew he would mingle with people who needed to invest money. His extraordinary networking approach was to avoid telling people what he did, and his wife also said very little to the other wives. Now I know what you're thinking. What was the point of it all if he was not prepared to say anything? Well, what he did was to say more on the last few days of the cruise. People then were so fascinated and impressed by this approach that when they handed over their business card to him, having got to know him really well, they would inevitably say, "Do contact me when we get back to London." This particular gentleman's career mushroomed as a result and five years later he retired in Spain at 48.

Networking as an art form

What an extraordinary world we live in today where technology is concerned. Maybe I'm giving my age away, but I'm invariably in awe of the 'techies' who visit my business to ensure our IT is up to date and working effectively. It used to be that as each year passed something new would come along; now it's more like as each month or even as each week passes, which is exciting and scary all at the same time.

Despite all this, I still have a networking encyclopaedia which I first started to build over a decade ago. My only regret is not having started it sooner, even though prior to this I always collected business cards and kept my contact diary as bulging as possible, which is always critical for sales success in financial services.

This networking encyclopaedia is different, however. I staple or glue the business card into the sizeable workbook and then write lots of notes next to the card based on the person I've just met, who he or she is, what they do, their children's names, the name of their pets and even if I've discovered they love chocolate. Also around the card I will write notes about who they know that I know, how I got to meet them in the first place and of course who they subsequently introduced me to.

Now I'm sure there's a technological way of doing the very same thing, but I have to say that there's something quite fascinating and right-brain creative about doing this exercise without technology. It allows you to pour over the pages from time to time, make links between different individuals and also give you the ammunition to make call backs to people you only met once and had they not been in the encyclopaedia, you probably would not have considered contacting them again.

This is the stuff that networking is made of. People often hold the idea of networking in their head as shaking hands and going to meetings, yet the basis of networking is the creation of a net, a place where you've captured people and their details and then go about working this to your advantage... in every way possible.

Like most things in this book it's highly mindset-related and I've done a great deal of networking by thumbing through my encyclopaedia and quite simply putting people together based on re-reading all the information I have about them. So if there were three steps in networking they would be:

1. **Create a net, a place where you capture people and information which you subsequently intend to work.**

2.   **Link people in your net together by your primary introduction.**

3.   **Go out into the big wide world and make more new contacts for your net on a regular basis.**

Step one is easy. It's the practicality of making this concept work. Step two is even easier and great fun to instigate. I love it when people ring me up and thank me profusely for an introduction to another business person. It's as if I've done some momentous act that they are deeply grateful for and by the way they invariably ask what they can do for me which is of course music to my ears.

It reminds me of the movie, *The Godfather,* where Marlon Brando would do favours for people and in return he would remind them that at some future point in time he may come knocking on their door. When you're running a business, it's sometimes life-saving to have favours owed to you by influential people. In order to have this facility, you need to network in the first place and do it well.

Looking at step three, this is the part that most people view as true networking. Yet on its own without the other two it's pretty sterile and tame at the best of times. In a real life situation if you meet someone at a business meeting and exchange cards, unless there's something you can immediately do together which is of equal importance, there's a disparity which often sabotages the exchange of business cards in the first place. In other words, if I meet someone and know that I could do a lot for them but have nothing to gain from the connection or it's the other way around, the chances are that one of us is going to be deeply disappointed. If however I recognise that the person I am being introduced to could be of tremendous help to me, I would not want to play my hand immediately; I'd want to capture the information and initially contact them with a third-party introduction as the first step. Of course I might then be a little cheeky and mention other ways we could work together bringing myself into the equation but at all times I will be tactful and undoubtedly very laid-back in my approach.

Something very tacky around networking is the discussion of commissions and introductory fees. To introduce two people and then attempt to do some sort of deal with both of them is most likely not only to fail, but blow up in your face. When networking it's not about percentages and fee splits, it's more about people helping each other, allowing each individual to make their own profit without having to involve each other around figures and percentages. This makes things clean, crisp and highly professional.

Casting your net

As an entrepreneur or small business owner, networking should be a strategic activity that you are regularly carrying out. Some of the places I network are:

- **professional industry meetings**
- **courses and workshops**
- **business presentations**
- **supplier meetings**
- **chamber of commerce**
- **health clubs and gyms**
- **aeroplanes and trains (while travelling business class)**
- **exhibitions and trade shows**
- **asking to be introduced to others by those already captured in your net.**

Dare I say, getting this book published was a networking exercise. It allowed me to send something quite unusual to people I knew as well as those I wanted to meet. Nothing sinister, simply a professional way of getting to know someone by allowing them to know all about you through the medium of a book. You can also use CDs, DVDs and the Internet if you can coax people to take a look at your site.

The other side of networking

Over time I've made many contacts, the majority of whom I've kept in touch with in one way or another, yet simply making that connection, logging it and doing some follow-up work is barely what networking is truly about. Good networking is creating a mini relationship with that individual or organisation to the point at which it's a two-way process rather than you always having to make the first move. So if you can get the other party to also want to keep the connection with you then you are building an arterial network, as it were, with you at the heart of it.

When I've attended networking meetings in the past I'm fascinated by the frenzied activity that takes place and the rapid exchange of business cards with the complete lack of relationship creation. Sometimes, I've observed two individuals talking at each other, making very little eye contact and probably already looking around the room for the next person they need to interact with. What's the point of having a dozen business cards in your pocket and not really knowing too much about these individuals when you can have two or three cards with people you've had meaningful interactions with who now all want to keep in touch with you and perceive you as much more than a chance business introduction who becomes purely another business card to record and keep and, dare I say, probably never contact ever again.

I suppose I've created a set of rules that I use when actually doing the networking in order to create relationships:

- **Eye contact without staring.**

- **Proactively listening with genuine interest.**

- **Ensuring that I am committing their Christian name to memory.**

- **Making the conversation interesting from my side.**

- **Working hard on establishing common ground.**

- **Thinking how I can help them in their business.**

- **Giving and taking business cards with respect.**

- **Being there in the moment with undivided attention.**

- **Anchoring the conversation with humour where appropriate.**

Isn't it curious here in the West how we very often treat our business cards like pieces of valueless paper. In the East, it can almost be a ceremony when business people exchange cards. My contention is that there is a happy medium to be observed around business cards and I suggest three simple rules:

1. **Handle your card and theirs with the greatest of respect.**

2. **When handed their card take a moment to read it properly and always flip it over in case there's something on the back.**

3. **Always be seen to be placing their card in an important place once it's in your possession.**

Cardinal sins around business cards include where you take the card and pop it in a pocket without even glancing at it, or sliding your card along the table to the person with one finger indicating very little respect for your own organisation. And in the same vein, throwing your card across the table in the same way you may dispose of a piece of unimportant litter which is of little value or surplus to requirements.

I also have a very simple rule about dealing with people's names. When meeting someone for the first time I will ensure I get their name right by using it in the first few moments of the meeting. During the conversation I will also ensure I use their name at least once and certainly no more than twice. Using a person's name incessantly whilst talking to them for the first time can sound very cheap and patronising, which I suggest should be avoided at all costs. Finally, I'll use the person's name right at the end of the interaction to end things on a sweet note. After all they do say that a person's name is, to them, the sweetest sound!

Follow-up networking

There are various ways I like to follow up my contacts. Mentally treating them all as friends is a good place to start. A lot of these events will have no particular reason attached and although this might sound like endless networking sessions, you probably know that the more you see someone the greater the likelihood is that mutual business will be transacted.

Probably a good way to switch your network contact off is to send them monthly newsletters from your organisation or reduce the relationship to a Christmas card every year. One of my own network contacts sends me 'thought for the month' rather than a newsletter which is a short, sharp yet fascinating nugget of information which I always look forward to receiving. Often when I receive it I'm prompted to pick up the phone and call them with a reaction. This gives both of us a chance to connect quite frequently and ensure the window of opportunity is always ajar.

Looking back at some of the most important things that have ever happened to my business, the majority of these wins are connected with someone I networked with in the first instance. The classic phrase, 'It's not *what* you know, but *who* you know' has always rung true for me, particularly in building the *Results Financial* organisation.

3. On the back of...

Many successful businesses realise that if they work with another business helping that business's client bank and perhaps do this with various businesses, they are going to see a rather sharp and rapid increase in business themselves. For example, as an adviser I often work on the back of the client base of solicitors, accountants and other professionals. Provided that the professional likes what I do and can see a link in terms of support services, they'll end up doing the marketing and advertising for me.

Often when I've mentioned this concept to other business owners their response is quite negative. They say things like, "Well, it'll probably work for you but my business is very different". Forgive me, but this is poppycock. All it says to me is this person lacks imagination and is not prepared to open their mind.

In recent times one of the most successful concepts came from Borders Book Shops. It realised that Amazon was steeling a march on them and they thought long and hard how to give their businesses, based in buildings rather than on the Internet, the edge. What could they do that Amazon couldn't?

Some bright spark came up with coffee shops.

They ended up doing an 'on the back of' deal with Starbucks where Starbucks would operate within their stores. They were climbing on the back of the Starbucks brand and existing success and getting Starbucks customers to come into their book stores while allowing their own customers to enjoy a coffee and spend more 'dwell time' in their book shops. Initially it seemed a rather strange idea and yet they had the courage to roll it out. Nowadays just about every major bookstore, including a more traditional WH Smith, has jumped on the band wagon.

4. Loyalty rewards

AirMiles, Nectar Points and other such loyalty reward schemes are big business. Of course the idea is nothing new and back in the 60s there used to be Green Shield Stamps.

Smaller businesses have credit-card-size bonus cards where your card is stamped every time you make a purchase. Full cards can then be exchanged for goods or services. There are various ways of rewarding customers and the question I put to you is – are you rewarding customers at all? And if not, why ever not?

I know today we're besieged by plastic cards being offered at petrol stations, supermarkets and chemists. All the major stores are offering loyalty points and very often you would need a separate wallet to carry all the cards around with you. So reward points are not the only solution. Writing or ringing up some of your customers sporadically to offer 'specials' might be the other way to go which I certainly find more preferable. This creates a more personal touch and undoubtedly loyalty. This could relate to a seminar, event or social gathering that's open only to a certain part of your clientele.

Putting on a special event and inviting the top 20% of your

customer base is a rather good way of bringing in fresh business. Provided any event is well attended, people get in the mood to buy. Such an event should also encourage the invitation of friends and family as new potential customers. Try and make the event unusual as something as boring as a coffee morning is unlikely to create a stampede.

5. Courtesy call

I remember taking my car in for a service last year and when I got home someone called from the garage to check I was happy. This made me smile as it was a nice gesture. Several months later when I took my car in again, I came home expecting the same thing but they never called.

So the most important thing about courtesy calls is *consistency*. To do it as a one-off and never do it again will do more harm than good. If your business is doing a yearly courtesy call, then one of the questions could well be: 'Is there anyone else you know who would benefit from our products or services?' Calls coming too often can also be counterproductive so a happy medium is key and this depends on the type of business you run.

6. Media publicity

It's surprising how much free media publicity is available to businesses, yet very few seem to take this option. I've enjoyed articles in magazines and journals which are in effect massive adverts and paid absolutely nothing for the privilege. Other avenues include radio and even the television.

I was stunned to see a London firm of financial advisers on an early morning breakfast show some time ago, and quite surprised. When I made further enquiries, I discovered that the reason they had such a fantastic prime time slot was because they contacted the TV station and simply suggested the idea! I was kicking myself.

Yet as I remember, viewers had assumed they were on television because they were such a top-notch firm. I also know that they transacted a large volume of business having been seen on television. The power of the media, indeed! The way to truly get media attention is to come at them from an unexpected angle. If it's unusual enough and interesting enough, they tend to invite you with open arms. This idea has the most potential and least competition. It simply requires confidence and boldness together with a half-decent idea.

Two publications I would recommend, which would highlight media contacts, are *The Writers' and Artists' Year Book* and *The Writer's Handbook,* both available from major book stores. These publications come out once a year and are well worth a look at when you are next browsing with your cup of coffee.

Every business needs a 'marketing engine', an engine that fires on four to six cylinders or four to six good prospecting ideas. If you've no engine or have less than four cylinders in operation then you're risking severe challenges and snarl-ups in your business and even, heaven forbid, a major breakdown. In order to stay well clear of such catastrophes, make it your priority to check out the state of your marketing engine in your business on a regular basis. Get this part right and you'll never look back.

Do not go where the path may lead, go instead where there is no path and leave a trail.

Ralph Waldo Emerson

7

Amazing Every Customer

It's such a really simple idea.

Treat your customer the way you would adore to be treated yourself, then go the extra mile and occasionally do something that takes them by complete surprise in a really positive way. That's it, there's your customer magic.

Businesses and corporate bodies around the globe eulogise about the importance of looking after your customers. The reality is something else again.

I once remember driving to a hotel in the Midlands where I was staying for one night. This hotel had been arranged by my office and I had never stayed there before. What was curious was the hotel's very explicit instruction on the entrance that I should drive through upon my arrival. As I approached the hotel I could see the way they wanted me to enter marked very clearly, so I pulled in off the road and into the gravel car park. No sooner had I turned off the engine and looked into my rear view mirror than I saw a member of the hotel in full crisp uniform approaching me quite smartly. The first thing that dawned on me was that I had chosen the wrong place to park and they were about to put me straight. Nothing could have been further from the truth.

"Mr Bell?" I peered out of my window and gazed at the smile of this well-presented beaming individual, a lady in her late forties.

"That's me."

Then it occurred to me, how did she know who I was?

"Do you have any luggage?"

I nodded, got out of my car and walked to the boot. As I opened it her hand moved in and took out my overnight case.

"Mr Bell, if you'd like to follow me?"

I grabbed my briefcase and locked the car before following her to the reception.

"Excuse me, have we met before?"

"I don't think so, and you're most welcome."

"It's just that you seem to know me."

The lady smiled but was clearly not about to give the game away, not quite yet. As I walked into reception the check-in process had already begun as I met with her colleague who had ensured that most of the information required for registration had already been taken by my office and completed on my behalf. My bag had already gone on ahead to my room as I simply completed the signature on the card. Once more the lady used my name as if we had known each other for years.

"I'm sorry, I'm trying to work out whether I've been here before, and as far as I'm aware I haven't."

"No, you're right there Mr Bell. Your office did say that this was going to be your first visit."

"So how do you know my name?"

The receptionist grinned, "We like to take a calculated risk."

Then she pointed to the security screen indicating where my car was parked.

"We get it from your registration number. As you enter it's logged and connected to our database of guests arriving - a simple method of deduction!"

Brilliant. And what a fantastic effect it had on me... This hotel had gone the extra mile and had offered me something quite surprising, and there were to be many more of these surprising processes they had put into place as part of their procedure of looking after their guests. Customer satisfaction? Not on your life, in fact even beyond customer delight.

In that particular month I must have shared that story more than a dozen times. I also know for a fact that two of my colleagues who heard this tale booked in there as a result of my recommendation. Not only did their system impress, it was strategic enough to make them money. As business guru Tom Peters always says, if your customer delight is off the scale, then you will never suffer the vagaries of famine and feast in your business. You will be feasting every day of the week.

The research speaks for itself. Businesses that really look the part with poor customer service suffer worse results than businesses that don't look particularly spectacular yet have the most extraordinary customer care values. Fortunately, it's the people element in a business's customer care programme that makes all the difference. I say fortunately, because less financial investment is required to create customer care processes that people of average ability then carry out. This is the great thing about extraordinary customer care in your business, you don't have to spend lots of money on technology or high salaries to achieve greatness. All you do need to do is have a sufficiently creative process that anyone with a modicum of intelligence can easily carry out.

In creating my own customer care experience – the magic, if you will – the starting place wasn't dreaming up what we'd do or even how we'd do it, it was about getting complete obsessive buy-in from every member of the team. I use the word 'obsessive' because it wasn't just about gaining commitment or support or even reminding my guys about the importance of teamwork. No, for this to work every member of the team would have to individually feel an obsession about making it work. There's a lot of mistrust around the word obsession. It's almost as if there's something unnatural about it, and yet we are all obsessive about at least one thing in life. It's just that we fail to recognise this pretty concrete fact. Furthermore, we conveniently forget to apply obsession to the most important things that matter to us. Of all the things worth being obsessed about in a business my humble view is that your customers should be your obsession of choice.

I can count on one hand the number of businesses I've ever encountered who are obsessive about getting it right for customers. This may indicate to you that it's harder than you might suppose to make obsession work. The fact is that once every member of the team declares their genuine interest in being really 'up for it' when looking after customers, their combined commitment normally equates to an obsessive policy in your business. The only downside about this strategy for customers, is where it's compelling for most of the team yet has a lacklustre for one or a tiny minority of the group. This can be very damaging indeed.

I experienced this as a visitor to Disneyworld. Their customer delight is legendary, literally the stuff dreams are made of. I had read and heard so much about them that I made it my mission to experience as much of the Disney magic as possible. Then on my first visit, one of the Disney team was clearly having a bad day and rather than be bowled over by their beautifully choreographed customer care, I instead experienced merely above-average service whilst purchasing my ticket. It was such a letdown!

This is why once you've got your buy-in in place, go for a few small wins rather than a whole raft of goodies that are more difficult and time-consuming to implement. Because behind obsession is consistency. I'm sure you've experienced a hotel, shop or other service business that regularly impresses you until one day they let you down. This is less likely to happen if you start with two or three great things that everyone can get right all of the time. One of these things in my business is the way the telephone is answered. There is a consistency and professionalism about it that many clients notice and appreciate. To start with it required a little bit of effort and practice, and after a few days it soon became a habit. The cost of implementation was virtually nil other than the time it took to coach the team and then ensure they were using it regularly. There's little excuse for any company not to be particularly good speaking to customers over the phone and yet those businesses that do get it right are once more in the minority.

I remember a Chinese restaurant delivery service who upgraded their service overnight. From no uniforms they went to crisp, bright, clean outfits which really represented their business. They introduced a scheme where they gave you a twenty-minute time period to expect the food. If they delivered beyond this time, they agreed that the food would be delivered without charge. There were a couple of other things they also decided to bring into force which soon made them the most popular fast-food delivery service in the area. As far as I'm aware, they are still in business and thriving.

A great way to begin the magic in your business, or indeed in anything you do for other people, is to ask lots of questions and find out what really works for customers. Getting an outside agency to collate this information is probably the best way to go, so that customers are happy to say absolutely anything when questioned. Running some sort of regular check-up system and comparing results from one month or quarter to another should also be someone's job in the team.

One very simple concept was explained to me early on in my business which really crystallised the strategic importance of a robust customer care process. Quite simply it was this: imagine drinking a cup of coffee and after every mouthful taking the cup back to the kitchen and decanting it in a fresh cup and saucer. The inconvenience and stress attached not to mention the sheer lack of enjoyment would all contribute to making this an expensive process. This analogy maybe applied to customer care. If there is no process and each customer care experience is based on ad hoc principles which may or may not work out, you're probably having to find another customer to replace the one you've just dealt with in order to keep the business moving. In other words separate mouthfuls of coffee in different cups. Now imagine creating such a rich meaningful and valuable customer experience that you know the customer will come back time and time again. Translated, the same coffee cup used effectively without the need for finding a new one.

The biggest 'monster' in customer care is perceived indifference. From a 1980s research project, perceived indifference was found to be the number one reason why most customers failed to return. The customers felt that the business couldn't really care whether they were customers or not.

The other thing I chose to do when setting up my business was conduct a brainstorming session with my business coach. We sat down in a hotel and put ourselves in the shoes of potential clients. I remember making a list of those things that I would fully expect from a company of the quality I planned to offer. It was a sobering yet quite exciting exercise and it was the launch pad to customer magic at *Results Financial*. Every so often I make it a business practice to revisit our customer offering and look at further ways of developing what we've created to stay one step ahead of the game.

If you look at any business, it's plain to see that the majority of new business always comes from existing happy customers. It is at least ten times easier to sell to an existing customer than to find a brand new one. So any business that's not saving customer data and linking it to marketing processes is simply making life infinitely tougher for itself. Special offers and equally special privileges should be regularly offered to your customer base and rather than not offering your customers attractive packages designed to bring in fresh enquiries, existing customers should be looked after infinitely better than the great customer care you levy for brand new buyers.

What the real magic is all about

I've frequently noticed that if you get customer care right you'll have them coming back time and time again, and naturally if you get it wrong you are unlikely to see the customer return. It's the vast 'middle area' I want to bring to your attention now. This 'middle area' is the kind of customer service that most businesses can offer consistently and yet fail to do so because either they are spending excessive amounts of time getting it completely right or completely wrong. Of course I appreciate in an ideal world it would be wonderful to get it completely right 100% of the time, yet surprisingly you often get customers withdraw from something that seems too good to be true, and because you're dealing with human beings it's unlikely that there is any formula that creates perfection for every customer every time.

So looking at the Customer Satisfaction Window, on one side you have the desire to create perfect service and on the other end of the scale we have unacceptable service. It's sad to say that there are infinitely more companies dishing out poor service than those striving to be the best.

So once more I ask you to consider the big area in the middle – the 80% area that too few businesses have a real grasp of. To give you a feel for what I'm talking about here I'd like to cite the example of a very well-known airline. I remember once travelling first class and sitting in the appropriate lounge. Just before my flight was called one of the cabin crew smartly dressed, approached me and checked my name. Once this was established he invited me to follow him as he was my escort to board the aircraft. Although this was a nice touch, and I could not fault the company in their grand scheme of creating 'the wow factor', I did notice that the next time I was flying that route first class, I chose another airline! The reason for this is difficult to explain.

I suppose that the nub of the experience I had with them was a dual band of ideas – the thought that I must have been paying for this extraordinary service and was it a good way to invest my contribution, and also it was a little over the top, perhaps. I remember being queue-jumped past lots of other economy and business class passengers and I did feel a little embarrassed if the truth be known. There would be many passengers who would love every minute, yet for me I was definitely 'an eighty percenter' rather than a top ten percent customer.

As strange as it may sound, the businesses that get 80% right are probably more successful than those businesses attempting 100% perfection. And because getting it completely right all of the time for all of the customers is a virtual impossibility, the 80% route saves time, money and is highly profitable.

I remember building a client bank once which became rather large and unwieldy. I had to make a decision about giving away some of my clients to members of my team. The nagging thought was – would they be as good with my clients as I knew I was myself. By letting go and trusting them to get it 80% right I ended up growing my personal production and business at the same time. By not having that faith and insisting that only I was good enough for my own clients, I wouldn't have the business that I enjoy today. So this was a big learning curve for me that getting it 80% right not only works and makes your company's service special, there is also the bandwidth within that 80% area to create some real magic with some simple, obvious and differential processes that will still get you talked about.

Turn your face to the sun and the shadows fall behind you.

Charlotte Whitton

8

The Challenge with Problems

Rather like decision-making, entrepreneurs appear to have no set process or solution for problem-solving. I first came across this obvious drawback when I became self-employed. In the early days, time and time again I would hear people come out with comments like "You seem to have a problem there," or "You have to sort that problem out before you can take it any further," and so on. I suppose it's a bit like saying to your children "Go and study for an hour," or "Do your homework," knowing that the young person in question has never undertaken any kind of coaching or tuition around study skills – and yet we are asking them to go off and make it up as they go along.

I often perceive this whole notion of expecting results without giving people tools as pure madness in the extreme. I, for one, would love to see the following new subjects taught at school *before* any academic pursuits: how to study, how to pass exams, how to revise, how to remember things and how to do your homework, etc. And so it is in business. "You have to make a decision about this and you have to sort that problem out."

It's perfectly true that problem-solving is often applied to situations in a business where there isn't in fact a problem in the first place. This is a good place to start. I remember watching a documentary on television about survival. Apparently some navies in the world have a survival guide with a golden rule that permeates all other instructions and suggestions for surviving. The golden rule is quite simply:

Whatever we do, say or propose during the time we are waiting to be rescued, the comment or suggestion must be optimistic.

On reflection this is good advice. If a group of survivors were to be thoroughly negative and pessimistic, it's unlikely they would have a good chance of survival and they would certainly miss that ship in the distance if they are not looking for it in the first place. It seems that some navies take things one stage further and suggest that anyone being negative would have to be removed from the survival raft and left to take their own chances! This seems a bit drastic and I can understand the thinking here. One bad apple in the barrel invariably destroys the rest. More about this later.

In a small business whatever problem comes your way, it has to be cut down to size at the earliest opportunity and certainly dealt with as quickly as possible. With the survival concept in mind, I would suggest that you deal with any problem with optimistic solutions first before anything else. Here are some questions you might wish to ask yourself when posed with a business problem regardless of size.

- **What could possibly be an upside to this problem?**

- **What could I learn from being able to resolve the problem?**

- **In the greater scheme of things is this problem actually a lot smaller than it really is?**

- **In resolving this problem effectively would it give me a wider breadth of experience as an entrepreneur?**

Dealing with problems at the earliest opportunity sounds obvious yet isn't it fascinating how many businesspeople set the problem to one side hoping that it might go away? I would agree that occasionally you can set a problem aside and it does resolve itself – though this is rarely the nature of a real problem. So doing something about it, taking action in other words, is pivotal if you are seeking an effective solution. It's hardly rocket science to realise that the longer you leave a problem, the greater the effort that will be required to achieve a desired solution.

I have often found the mere fact that I have taken action – for example, picked up the phone, drafted an email or written a letter – has kick-started the journey to resolution and invariably that within that action the solution is hiding.

Inside out

Have you ever found the solution to a problem at a time when you least expect it? This happens to most people – while driving a car, watching television, having a meal, chatting to a friend or that classic eureka moment in the bath. With this in mind one of my favourite ways of problem-solving is using a technique called *Fast-Forward.*

Fast-Forward is having a conversation with somebody (this may even include the cat!) as if you are at some point in the future. In other words you fast-forward time and talk historically about having solved the problem. Although this technique sounds somewhat strange to say the least, it really does work. What happens is you relax and enjoy discussing how the solution came about and rather like sitting in the bath or watching television, the right side of your brain – the creative side – inevitably comes into play. It's extraordinary that using this methodology you often come out with the answer you were looking for because the process has no stress or pressure around it. There have been occasions when I have been utterly astounded by what comes out of this surreal conversation, which is exactly the right solution for the issue being discussed.

If you're wondering how far into the future you should go, this will depend on the nature of the problem and how serious it is. Small issues may only require you being 24 hours into the future where larger issues might require a week or even a month. Deadlines will also govern the timescales you choose. The advantage of this Fast-Forward technique is that it may be used on your own, with someone else or with a large group of people. It can also be a lot of fun, though unnecessary or inappropriate humour needs to be avoided as this can be a distraction to discovering your solution.

That's ridiculous

The other thing I've been shown to do is to construct a RIDICULOUS LIST.

As the term suggests, a ridiculous list is making an extensive note of 'ridiculous' solutions. These may be as ridiculous as you choose and the apparent madness of this method is precisely what's required in order to often come up with something that, on the face of it, appears ridiculous and yet on second analysis could actually be exactly what you're looking for.

I remember a few years ago taking exactly this approach when looking for a resolution for a new office. Given that my industry is financial services and not high street retail, the idea of being based in a shop was in many ways quite ridiculous. Given that our clients tend to come from personal recommendation and introductions from other professionals, the last thing we'd require is a high street presence or a shop window. Yet on closer analysis of this so-called ridiculous solution there were so many advantages we'd never considered before. And now *Results Financial* is proudly situated at 656 Chesterfield Road in Sheffield. And yes we've even had business from people walking in through the door, which I've certainly never experienced before in decades of being a financial adviser.

The live brainstorm

Too often we want to hold on to our problems and issues rather than share them. Sharing in my view is a very good way of dealing with problems, particularly the bigger ones. It's interesting that we all have solutions to problems that are not ours. It's always easier to solve someone else's problems rather than our own. The personal attachment around a problem can often close our eyes to the obvious.

The best way to share a problem in terms of resolving it is through a brainstorm. Now simply getting people sitting around a table is not necessarily the way to go, here. I've found that the session needs to be formal and should start with ten minutes of brainstorming of each attendee on their own before they join the main session. This means that when the main brainstorming commences people have in front of them lots of suggestions to get the ball rolling. Any brainstorming session should have someone heading or leading the group, someone separate to write down what's being said on a flipchart and a third individual to keep an eye on the time so that the meeting has some parameters. Often the shorter the meeting is, the more effective the process becomes. You may also wish to consider an extremely short and sharp brainstorming session that lasts a mere ten minutes where everyone stands rather than sits around the flipchart, which tends to give the session more energy and adrenalin.

Once more I would encourage the use of mind maps where

appropriate for thinking outside the box or capturing thoughts and ideas. I'd also use colour where possible as this has strong creative overtones.

I was once having a conversation with a fellow businessman who remarked that his definition of heaven was a place where there were no problems. My first instinctive reaction was to agree with him until I thought about it some more. To me a life without problems would initially sound wonderful, and yet surely after a while life would get very boring. Though none of us wants problems, it is nevertheless great to be able to deal with them in a positive way and create positive resolutions that allow us to step back and feel good about our endeavours. Similarly with a small business, if you've built something over the years that has taken you on a bit of a rollercoaster ride, which includes small, medium and large problems, ultimately when you look at your baby fully grown there has to be a momentous feeling of pride and fulfilment that you attribute to your courage and optimism.

Problems are here to stay, whether it be in our life or our business, and the test we put ourselves through is whether we have the resolve and positive mental attitude to step up to the plate, take action and celebrate a great result.

You cannot discover new oceans unless you have the courage to lose sight of the shore.

9

Product Love Affair

It was a cold winter's evening and I gingerly stepped out of my car onto six inches of snow. Carefully I made my way to the front door of an old school friend who had rung me recently and asked me to look at an amazing business opportunity.

I was quite excited because I am one of these individuals who like to think they have an extremely open mind and I'm always on the lookout for something that makes sound business sense. As the door opened and I stepped inside the warm hallway, I could hear the buzz of voices, clearly indicating that there were several people already here. At seven the event got underway and within ten brief minutes I realised I was in the middle of a sales presentation. Forty minutes later, products appeared ranging from cleaning materials to jewellery and health products. If you haven't already guessed I was being subjected to some multi-level marketing.

Since the late 70s there have been umpteen organisations, many of which originate from the USA, who come across to our shores with the very latest scheme to make lots of money. I have to say that there's little doubt that these schemes could well make you rich, yet the reality is that only a tiny proportion make it and the rest muddle through for a while or give up after a relatively short period.

As I listened to the marketing plan, I had to admit that it was appealing. It had been well thought through and did make business sense albeit in theory. Eventually my friend cornered me and asked me for a candid response to his question as to whether I was interested. I paused and smiled at him. I could tell he was desperate to sign up as many people as possible that evening, yet I do tend to be an individual who speaks his mind and doesn't fudge issues. I placed a hand on his shoulder and in a kindly manner indicated that this wasn't really my cup of tea. Disappointed, he asked me why, and I explained to him that as much as it appeared to be a great marketing plan, I could not get very excited about selling cleaning products and jewellery, whether it be directly or on an indirect basis.

If there's one thing I've learned over the years as an entrepreneur, it is that whichever product or service you sell you have to live, eat, breathe and love with a passion. As indicated in an earlier chapter, I would even go further to suggest that if there is no passion you won't have a business for very long. Over the decades I've seen time and time again individuals who get excited about setting up their own business based not on the product or service but based on the figures and the plan to get rich. You don't have to be a behavioural psychologist to know when someone is selling something to you because they want to make a sale, or when they are selling something that they genuinely feel would add value to your life. I certainly find it very difficult to say no to something of the latter quality. When I'm shopping around I normally end up dealing with a supplier who has passion about what they're selling, even though it might be a little bit more expensive, rather than deal with something 'cheap and cheerful' from an individual who's keen to grab my credit card.

And so I turn my attention to you, the reader. Let me ask you candidly: How passionate are you about your product and/or service? Furthermore, how much do you believe in your product and/or service and how passionate do you get when you share your sales proposition with someone else?

When I first started selling financial services I was very excited. I genuinely went out into the world passionate about the concept of life assurance and what it could do for families and individuals in just about every walk of life. There's no question that people bought from me because of my passion and you may already know that most people buy emotionally not logically. This should doubly emphasise to you that passion helps you to sell whilst at the same time assisting people to buy.

One of the challenges around passion is getting other people in your organisation to feel how you feel. Some of the ways of making sure that you and your colleagues are aligned include:

- **Asking good questions at the person's initial interview.**

- **Having regular reviews which touch on the importance of being passionate about your products and services.**

- **Making sure your training around products and services is always up to date and conducted in a positive, exciting manner.**

- **That you buy, and are seen to buy, your own products and services at all times. It's like the well-known example of the restaurant manager going out for lunch. We also all remember the Gerald Ratner story and how his empire fell apart when he made his quip about his products being rubbish. Okay, it may have only been a joke – but an expensive one.**

The great thing about passion is that it's almost impossible to fake. Passion comes from a genuine, positive feeling and will be seen in your smile, be heard in your words and be felt in the sentiments you express. Also it's worth bearing in mind that the more passion that exudes from individuals around products and services, the less overselling need be done in front of customers. When you are truly passionate about what you do, products tend to sell themselves.

So what do you do if passion is lacking in your business around products and services? Here are some suggestions:

1. Run a customer advisory clinic

This could be operated by your accountant or a management consultant who invites a cross-section of your customers and suppliers into a brainstorming session around your products and services. My feeling is that every business should do this anyway, and it really does help to identify what's missing in what's being sold in your organisation. Often the information is dynamite, and I suggest that you ensure you stay well away from the session itself. People tend to open up about you and your company if you are not there to hear what they have to say. Hopefully a lot of it will be good and you must be brave enough to take any negativity on the chin on the basis that this will help you do something about it.

2. Internal brainstorm

How regularly do you review your products and services internally? Making the assumption that the product you've had for a couple of years will still be good for another couple of years can often be the first nail in a coffin. I always remember the Swiss watch industry story where the Swiss watch industry turned down the idea of a battery-operated watch because it didn't fit within their beliefs around how watches should be made. They ended up losing their large market share lead and currently struggle to export their products in comparison with what's happening with other countries in the world.   It's a fact that consumers do get bored with products which fail to keep abreast of the times.

Another good example is the mobile phone industry. Every six months a new model phone comes out with even more features and benefits. Imagine if this industry failed to change and were less than passionate about continually giving customers the best product. It would probably mean we'd still all be carrying around those massive phones which were as heavy as a brick that came out in the mid-80s. Heaven forbid!

3. Use the alternative SMART formula

I remember my business coach showing me an alternative to the well-known fifty-year-old **SMART** formula. The original formula stands for **S**pecific, **M**easurable, **A**chievable, **R**ealistic, **T**imed.

Now consider an alternative. How about **S**pecial, **M**assive, **A**wesome, **R**idiculous, **T**oday?

In considering your product and/or service, use this alternative **SMART** formula to check where you are with what you sell. In other words, does your product for example have a special quality? Does it have mass or massive appeal to customers? (If not what could you do about it?) Is it a product with great 'wow' potential – in other words is it awesome? Once again if it's not what could you do about this? Have you thought of how you could improve it in a way which currently might appear 'ridiculous'? And finally, what could you do about it today? In other words what immediate action are you prepared to take?

Passion is a great driver for any individual. We know that people are often passionate about their hobbies. It is so true that we tend to be much more knowledgeable about something we do for pleasure than the very professions we've been trained in. I know a doctor for example who is extremely satisfactory in all she does, yet her passion for classical music has made her a real expert in that field. Dare I be so bold to say that she likes practising medicine and yet is not as passionate about it as she is with classical music. I remember asking her why she had not made music her vocation. She smiled and said she couldn't see how it would pay the bills. Ah yes, that's a common response and often an issue around self-confidence.

Some time back, before I set up *Results Financial*, I took myself away to a hotel for the day and had a meeting with myself. This sounds completely bizarre and yet was one of the most valuable days I've had in a long while. I started the meeting with a blank sheet of paper, and then wrote down the things that I was most passionate about in life. Some of the things on my list included giving value to other people, running a business I would enjoy every day and spending time in the sun. Of course there were other smaller items but it was the big items that came through and helped me mould my life and business together as one entity.

Doing what I love is rather like getting paid to enjoy yourself seven days a week. For many people their mindset dictates that it is not possible to get paid for enjoying yourself on a day-by-day basis. May I respectfully suggest that this is a fallacy, a paradigm that is simply not true. My belief is that there are a lot of lazy individuals in the world who are not prepared to do the research and spend the discovery time that, if invested, could change their life forever.

For the true entrepreneur, having fully appreciated the importance of passion for what you love, the trick is adapting the concept for your products and services in a meaningful way which gives you a real opportunity to steal a march on the competition. In order to make it easy to feel passionate about your products or services, your offering should not be just a good one; it needs to be an extraordinary one. For those clients who find it useful, here at *Results Financial* we have an option to create a 'moneymap' for people's personal finances. We even have a moneymap version for small businesses. This concept is highly original and currently is certainly not being offered by other competitors.

For members of the team, our package to financial advisers who join *Results Financial* is extremely attractive. It's interesting how I get comments from other businesses in our industry asking the question as to how I could possibly make any money charging such low fees. When you put your customer first – in this case financial advisers – financial considerations normally take care of themselves.

I will continue to be passionate about my business, my life, the people around me and an endless stream of opportunities that snake into the future. Where success is concerned passion isn't an option, it's a necessity.

**Where there is no vision
the people perish.**

Solomon, Proverbs 29:18

$$\overline{\underline{10}}$$

Back to the Future

There are four things which over the years have been indelibly etched in my mind from the extraordinary and sometimes 'jumping in at the deep end' experiences I received early on in my career in the early 80s. 'Jumping in at the deep end' was definitely the case for anyone entering financial services who sought an opportunity to create a business from scratch. Today I reflect on many of my colleagues at the time who found themselves in one of two camps: those who were real entrepreneurs and sought to take full advantage of what was possible, and those who adopted a more timid stance and dare I say, were part of a group of people who left the industry early and who never really made the most of their opportunities.

It's the first group I want to draw your attention to, particularly if here today you would love to know the bottom line: what is the essence of being a true entrepreneur? Given that we are unable to go back in time, my offer to you in this chapter is to go back through my memories and experience and then into the future with some hot tips for your success.

1. Selling is the most important thing you can do

Back in the 80s I once went with a client to open a business bank account as she wanted to set up her own kindergarten. Mary was a friend of the family and she was keen to do all the right things for her first-time business venture. Once we got into the bank and in front of the bank manager it soon dawned on me that Mary had absolutely no idea about the nature of a business. She was applying for overdraft facilities in order that she could receive a wage for the next six months and her allocation to sales and marketing was to be negligible. When I queried this with her she explained that she was a good networker and a couple of mothers had already enquired as to when she was opening for business. As we left the meeting and strolled down the street the 'clincher' in the conversation was when she turned to me and said, "It's a good job there's no selling involved in my business – I'd really hate the idea". This was at a time when my experience of business was still an adventure for me too. Today, I would tell it how it is and ensure no one believes they can start a business and spend most of their time doing administration and hoping the selling will take care of itself.

Mary lasted her six months and managed to go ten months before she had to shut her doors and admit failure. She went back into employment with a rather negative experience behind her and an even more negative figure in her business account which she was given three years to repay.

In financial services in the 80s, sales was the key to everything. Though most advisers were self-employed they were in fact running their very own micro-businesses within a larger one. I was in no doubt that unless focus and attention was paid to good consistent selling underpinned by good sound marketing, my classic entrepreneur's comment applied – you didn't have a business, you had a job! I always smile when I watch programmes like *Dragons' Den*. So-called entrepreneurs come on the programme and stand there serious-faced requesting a large chunk of money to allow them to give up their day jobs! What's painfully obvious to the true entrepreneur is that most of these individuals have no stomach for taking a risk. It truly is about appreciating the difference between running a business and holding down a job. Inherent in the entrepreneurial risk comes immense opportunity. Of course it would be a much more attractive proposition if there was no risk at all. Then you'd have a situation where everyone would choose to be an entrepreneur, which can of course be immensely more exciting than being employed.

- **In my early career all the main factors were in place.**

- **I was prepared to take a risk.**

- **I understood that speculation attracted opportunity.**

- **I made myself accountable for my results.**

- **I put sales as the number one 'must have' on my agenda.**

- **I was fully aware that sales without marketing equals sand in your three-litre engine.**

2. Persist, persist and then persist some more

Back in the 1980s one of the best things to happen to the life assurance industry was the myriad of high-quality motivational speakers who shared their passions with other people. Some of the most inspirational were themselves in financial services, whilst others came from industries located far and wide. A story doing the rounds, which even today I find fascinating, is the story of Thomas Edison and his invention of the electric light bulb. Every time I hear the story the actual number of times Edison attempted to find his solution is different! Yet the consensus of opinion is that he did over a thousand experiments before he could shout eureka. Even if we were to take into account exaggeration and say that his experiments were merely a hundred in total, it's still very impressive. The story goes that he experimented time and time and time again with his friends and advisers telling him he was in fact wasting his time. Yet I wonder how long it would have taken someone else to come along had he given up before he achieved his greatness. Twenty-five years ago persistence appeared to be a much stronger force to be reckoned with. Today I notice young people looking for the easiest solution rather than one that would serve them well. Human patience appears to be at an all-time low where here in the West we tend to expect convenience everywhere we look. As an entrepreneur, if you know what you truly want and you've created a roadmap to get there, then persistence is your fuel which always guarantees arriving at your destination.

On one of these lunchtime presentations by a top industry speaker I listened as he explained to the audience the power of mathematical certainty.

"Take an apartment block with a hundred apartments. Imagine for a moment that it's early evening and eighty of the apartments have at least one occupant. Let's now arm you with a small case of polish and dusters and suggest that you knock on all one hundred doors asking each occupant the question – *would you like to buy a cheap polish and duster set?* So what response do you think you'd get in terms of sales?"

When I first heard this my immediate reaction was to think how lucky I was to be selling a great product. The idea of selling polish and dusters had to be way down an entrepreneur's choice of products. The speaker then came back with his answer.

"Of the one hundred doors you knock on, and the eighty that open the door to you, one individual will definitely buy and if you use some sales techniques with it you could end up with as much as three sales. The one sale however is based on mathematical certainty. However, to achieve mathematical certainty you would have to knock on all one hundred doors. If you were to knock on merely ninety then the certainty vanishes."

Not being a mathematician, I had no idea whether this was true or not, though I can attest to the fact that the more persistent I was about, for example, filling my diary to see new clients or calling existing clients to find out if they needed anything else, the greater my success. What this means is that persistence will ultimately allow you to find just about anything you're looking for in life. This is excellent news in running your own business because in a strange sort of way it removes the risk factor that daunts so many would-be entrepreneurs. So in order to make ten sales a day with your polish and duster set, you'd have to find ten apartment blocks with at least a hundred dwellings and ensure you visit them at the right time of day. With ten sales a day coming through regularly you can now start to equate a sales plan for yourself and possibly others.

This is the nature of computer spam. It's a great way to harvest mathematical certainty in selling. Of course, like most people I hate receiving spam on my computer and certainly would never wish it on anyone. It is, however, a really good example of how this principle works. If, like the spammers, you're prepared to persist unflinchingly until you achieve your goal, the fact is you probably will.

3. Never be 'fobbed off'

Early in my career I reflected how lucky I was to have a product that I could actually sell to anyone. If what I was selling was double glazing or kitchens for example, I'd automatically be streamlining my quest for customers with a smaller very specific group of individuals, individuals who owned their own property, rather than my great entrepreneurial opportunity of viewing everyone as a 'suspect'. With this firmly in my mind the world was my oyster and I got used to the idea of not necessarily taking 'no' for an answer. In fact as part of my training it was drummed into me that in the world of selling life assurance 'no' was often merely a 'yes' in disguise. This created a wry smile across the face of my other half who brought it to my attention that surely this was the epitome of selling such an unpopular product.

At this time I also read in a newspaper of a man selling double glazing who arrived at 5 pm to see his potential customers in their home, and at 1.30 am was still going for the close, refusing to budge from his seat in their front room until they signed on the dotted line. Apparently at 2.00 am the police arrived, and as he was being ushered out he even queried whether the policeman owned his own property!

With this firmly in mind, I need to explain that 'not being fobbed off' is not quite the same thing that I have in mind. It's more about being resistant to anyone attempting to derail you and put you on a completely different track. A better example in my career was wanting to sell a company pension scheme, yet not having the experience or knowledge to do so. I requested the assistance of a junior manager to go with me on the call. On the day of the meeting we agreed to rendezvous in his office and then we would walk the short distance to the company concerned. When I arrived my colleague was busy on the phone and he looked up at me somewhat concerned. Apparently there were certain matters he now needed to get done that morning and he politely suggested that we rearrange the meeting with the client for another day. Along with the suggestion, he advised me that on reflection Monday was never a good day to discuss company pension schemes and any other day would be more appropriate. I simply looked at him in sheer amazement. Here was a man who was certainly on my tail regarding results and production and yet now, because it didn't suit him, he wanted me to postpone something that had already taken much effort to arrange. Despite being new to the company I refused to budge and smiled back saying, "If we don't go today I fear we're going to miss the boat. I already know he has two more insurance companies to see this afternoon". That morning we both walked into the offices of a small but growing business and started the wheels in motion of a company pension scheme that was eventually completed fourteen days later. The total business was a worthwhile exercise for all concerned, not least the assistant manager's share.

As an entrepreneur it's so easy to be pulled off course by all manner of interferences. The potential list of culprits includes friends, family, colleagues, clients, professional advisers, television, radio, newspapers, what you were taught at school and so on.

Once more here was a tool that shaped my future and over the years that followed, never being fobbed off by anyone paid off many more times than it ever let me down. I also believe that any good entrepreneur's heart is located in their stomach. They have a feel for what's right and worth pursuing – gut instinct in other words. Stick with your true feelings, stand your ground and keep a hold of your dreams.

4. Write down what works, and what doesn't work

When I first started in financial services I was so focused on getting the business that inevitably I wasn't watching how I got from A (speaking to the prospect) to Z (taking the order and submitting it for underwriter approval). People used to ask me how come I was so successful, and I never used to give it much thought until one day I went through a bad patch where prospects were now saying 'no' to me alarmingly often. Yet as far as I was concerned I wasn't doing anything differently. It was then that it hit home that I wasn't fully aware of what had been working for me – the things I desperately needed to replicate at this time.

We all have a whole host of skills, many of which we take for granted. The new 'science' of NLP or Neuro-Linguistic Programming encourages the study of performance, noting specifically what people do in a skill situation to attain their success, and then getting others to replicate exactly the same thing. Back then, not fully appreciating NLP, I used to come out of a successful meeting and make a few notes of what precisely I did in what order. I then used to concentrate on replicating the things that were common in all my successful meetings, only to realise that I had created a blueprint a short while later which just about worked every time it was deployed.

Successful entrepreneurs the world over use the same process to consistently create success in their products and services, systems and processes. By making a note of what does work and equally what doesn't, this invaluable research information gives you the key to the door of positive and consistent outcomes.

Some people keep journals and today you could even keep a blog. In fact that very idea is something I will probably progress to, although have already begun through writing this book. Here' s hoping my contribution positively affects your current business and/or your future business to be.

**The price of greatness
is responsibility.**

Winston Churchill

11

The Hands of Time

Earlier I mentioned the importance of time and timing. Now I'd like to explore time and the entrepreneur in a little bit more detail.

When I was four years old my father decided to take a nap, and he put a clock in front of me and asked me to wake him after an hour. Taking him at his word I sat bolt upright with the alarm clock in front of me and I focused all my attention on the minute hand until I could actually see it moving. For one whole hour I did nothing other than watch time pass and sixty minutes later I woke him.

This is my earliest memory of my study of time. The most valuable resource we all have and yet fail to appreciate and correctly utilise. I remember what struck me as I watched the minute hand is that on careful observation you can indeed see it moving, though normally it appears motionless. In recent years I'm convinced it moves even faster than it ever has before; years seem to move at a lightening pace. No sooner has Christmas finished than Spring is upon us, and before you know it you're enjoying your summer holiday watching children get back to school then observe restaurants booking for the festive season.

So how does an entrepreneur really use time advantageously? There is of course no right or wrong answer here, though everyone would agree the question of how to get more out of your twenty-four hours a day is continually being asked. Time management courses the world over continue to offer time-saving tips and more effective ways of doing things. Ultimately we all have a choice either to ignore time at our peril and hope we still manage to get everything done that we need to, or to raise our hands and become willing to explore ways of genuinely cramming more into our days without the stress and with the rich rewards of being effective.

The Entrepreneur's Time Tool Kit

Wouldn't it be great for me to unveil an entrepreneurial time tool kit? Download a number of amazingly simple yet effective ways of being able to do more with your time? All I can say is, if you have such information that genuinely works I'd pay a lot of money for it. What I do have, through my years of experience in the world of business, is a list of suggestions which have worked for me and I trust will benefit you in some way.

1. Time Respect

If you respect time, time respects you. It's as simple as that. Respect for time to me means appreciating its speed and brevity, being on time for others and messaging other people, albeit politely, that they should respect my time. Where circumstances and engagements are important I also respect being on time to the extent of building in time pockets to cope with the unexpected. Surely it's disrespectful to leave your office on what is normally a one-hour journey with the full expectation that today the journey time will be as predicted leaving nothing to chance. Yet people do this time and time again and it's particularly embarrassing if the meeting is important and/or it's with a paying client.

2. Time Pockets

I've already mentioned building in time pockets to ensure you are in the right place at the right time. Conversely, what happens if you've built in time pockets and you get to your destination early and there's still twenty minutes before the start of your meeting. Would this not be a waste of time, particularly if you were doing this on a regular basis? Being prepared to deal with excesses of time or 'time pockets' is a real win for not just entrepreneurs but any human. My recipe is to always carry things with me that I can read or do. Today with the advent of the super-slim laptop we really have no excuse around wasting time. To be able to pull out your laptop at any time, anywhere, any place, and get some work done in a small eleven-minute time pocket is not only respectful of time but an excellent example of true personal effectiveness.

Of course I'm not suggesting you become boring and that every moment of your life is used to create something or complete a work-related task. I'm simply making the point that there are opportunities to maximise your time if you chose to do so.

3. Down Time

I always think that down-time is merely 'up time' in disguise. Translated – taking time off to recharge your batteries is good for you and should be done in small quantities throughout your year. What never works is the lack of planning around quality down-time in your year. The result of this negligence is down-time of a different nature where you are physically unwell and have no choice but to down tools until you recover. More and more these days I'm building in healthy amounts of down-time in my year. Indeed, as I grow older I think it vitally important to cash in and enjoy quality time as many times as my diary will permit. This I see as one of the immense rewards that entrepreneurship can bring.

4. *Time System Magic*

As humans we're all different and we view time in different ways. This also accounts for why some of us enjoy electronic time-planning devices whilst others are strictly paper-based system junkies who refuse to step into the twenty-first century. I believe there's a case for both and possibly the paper-based system with some electronic back-up. The main reason why I'm passionate about having a paper-based system is that it really suits the entrepreneur's mindset. With paper you can still be more creative and until technology tips the scales in the opposite direction I will advise a system that looks more like a Filofax and less like a mobile phone.

Once your chosen system is in place, of course, you have to use it. How you lay it out is largely up to you and will probably depend on trial and error before you have the final process that works. One little tip is to re-evaluate this whole idea of 'to do' lists. My coach gave me this tip-off that 'to do' lists can often become an excuse to park things unnecessarily, offering you stress and a growing mound of items which never seem to get done. Rarely do I ever hear people saying to me that their 'to do' list was done today and they really can't think of anything else to put on it anymore.

So here's the idea:

By all means have a 'to do' list but only add items to it which are non-critical, non-crucial, non-important items as opposed to strategic things that need to be done as quickly as possible. Now put all strategic and important items in your diary rather as you would put appointments into it. When you come to that item during your working day – just do it.

So what about the 'to do' list? Well, surprise surprise because it only contains things which are not important, it grows and festers and invariably as time passes you will realise that most of these things should not have been put on the list in the first place.   Just imagine if you had completed those items you would have spent valuable time on them only to realise that they were not that important at all!

So the bottom line is that time needs to be a factor that's taken into account with everything you do and should be ignored at your peril.

**You always miss 100%
of the shots you don't make.**

12

I'm Feeling Lucky...

I used to believe in luck, along with many people around me, and there came a point in my life where I made an important discovery: that whether you believe in it or not, you'll be right. Consequently, I decided to drop the belief and install a completely new one: that in order to be entirely successful and happy with your life you should go out and make it happen. The real challenge I've had with believing in luck is inevitably playing the waiting game. If you're waiting for luck to find you, then quite often it's a passive pursuit rather like waiting for that ideal month, year or day when it's time to improve your life, start a business or do something bold and magical.

The three components that have made a big difference to me, which seem to attract comments from others such as, "That was lucky," or "If you fell into the sea you'd come out bone dry, Michael," make up the words 'I AM': **I** = **I**nspiration, **A** = **A**ttitude, **M** = **M**otivation.

I like to remember these three ingredients because we were born with them hence the words 'I AM'. Yet when you look at the three elements more closely you will see that there are real subtle differences that need to be observed. Inspiration is something you often get from other people; attitude is what you do with the inspiration you've received; and finally, motivation is the consistent and continual driving force that never tires and propels you towards your goals and objectives in life.

Inspiration

Over the years I've taken my inspiration from a whole host of different individuals right across the globe. In the business and industry I chose, we pride ourselves on being one of the very few professions that helps to inspire each other along the way. For us, it's less about competition and more about support and genuine mutual assistance. In setting up your own business in your own industry I would suggest that much inspiration can be gained from those individuals who are already making a great success of what you also intend to be good at. It's curious how different cultures have different views on what inspiration truly is. I've noticed, for example, that in the Asian culture they have no fear in setting up businesses next door to each other. They tend to be inspired in terms of what they can achieve and also following role models who are out there doing well and making a fortune. In the West, particularly in the UK, we inevitably want to take competition into account and lack inspiration when we see others in our industry doing so well.

Early on in my professional career I made it my business to listen to and spend time with those entrepreneurs who were focused, driven and unstoppable. I've also made it my business over the years to travel the globe often to listen to specific individuals for maybe no more than an hour. Yet sitting and being inspired by these world-class success stories, and the copious notes I inevitably make as I listen to their ideas and thoughts intently, are worth all the effort and financial investment I made in the first place. As I for one know, my current success has been enhanced and accelerated by all of those individuals' input, and if I could go back a few decades the only change I would make is to spend even more time being inspired in such a way.

Other ways to source inspiration are from books, CDs, DVDs and the Internet, as I have mentioned before. Sometimes you can achieve a huge lift from a simple quotation or a chance remark from telephoning a business colleague or associate. Although I'll be looking at motivation separately (the **M** of 'I AM'), I would like to add that if ever I am feeling like a motivational boost I pick up the phone and I speak to a friend. Now I'm sure, as you will imagine, not every friend is there to support and help motivate you. In fact, the opposite is often true. Sometimes they will take the opportunity of downloading all their current negative baggage and if you're not careful you can get sucked in and actually believe what they're saying is true.

You may be wondering how this can be inspiring and ironically it is. When I listen to some people's tales of woe I also pick up the fact that their complaints are often quite trivial compared with what else is happening in the world. It also makes me feel good that I have developed a mindset to deal with challenges regardless of what they are. If we live our lives in a giant schoolroom, then we're here to learn lessons. If we learn by these lessons, they are rarely ever repeated though it is true that we move on to new lessons. For many people they go through the same lessons time and time again and decide to bring in other factors such as luck, which they use to avoid blame whilst extricating themselves from personal responsibility.

Attitude

Many years ago I was sitting next to a somewhat rotund American gentleman with a white beard and moustache who would be the splitting image of St Nicholas AKA Father Christmas. Yet this individual had a whole host of presents rather like his fantastical counterpart. It's from him that I remember what attitude is all about. Even though I never learned it from him, I did know some background about this gentleman. You would never have thought it, but he had a great deal to be miserable about. His son was disabled and could barely speak or see. His wife was in and out of hospital desperately fighting a serious ongoing illness and he had gone through additional personal trauma himself too sad to really go into in any detail.

Nevertheless, there I was sitting, sharing a coffee with him at an industry conference. His smile was infectious and he almost carried an aura that you could touch with your hands. What was so wonderful was the feeling of calm mixed with hope and tinged with excitement for the future. When I told him what my plans were for building a business of my own, he could only see success and gently but firmly spurred me on before it was too late. "Attitude plus latitude equals altitude." When he said these words, I smiled. Then I had to pull out my diary and write it down. He went on to explain that if you think in the right way and you broaden your horizons (hence the 'latitude') you attain altitude, or in other words you start to fly. Had anyone told me about this without meeting this amazing gentleman, I might have been tempted to smile and think it was all rather cheesy.

Yet here was the living, breathing embodiment of someone who had chosen the right attitude which enabled him, because of his mental flexibility and openness to the limitless possibilities we have in our lives, to fly over the storms in his life rather than straight through them.

Then he said the most amazing thing to me: "Michael, do you know you're one of the few people who really inspires me?" When I first heard him say this I grinned, assuming there was something ironic or even mildly sarcastic by the remark. How could I inspire someone like him? Then he went on to say how whenever we'd met before, I invariably wrote down something triggered in the conversation which almost made him feel privileged to be genuinely helping a fellow colleague and human being. "You know, Michael, I'm also inspired by the look in your eyes. When I talk to you your eyes are wide open, they're non-judgemental and they are full of hope for the future."

I was to meet him again just one more time the following year, as six months after that his life was ended by a brain tumour. If I was to describe my current attitude as a physical structure, then he's the foundation upon which everything else rests. The inspiration he gave me over the short time we knew each other became the bedrock for my way of thinking and my method of translating all negativity into something malleable that could be changed and reconstructed in a positive and meaningful new mental image.

After all we are all born with a facility called 'attitude'. This is like a house we live in or a suit we wear. And rather like a house or a suit, we can choose to present ourselves based on what we do with these items. It's my chosen belief that what you live in and what you wear is a reflection of how you think. You don't have to live in a palace or have a hand-tailored garment to be successful. It's the chosen attitude that goes with these things that creates the true reflection of who you are along with all the seeds of potential for a successful future.

In an earlier chapter I mentioned that some navies would favour forcible removal of negative thinkers from survival rafts. The following story explains why this might be the case.

About twenty years ago an American naval ship sank in the Pacific Ocean. In this major disaster there were two life rafts with occupants about half a mile apart. On the first raft there were eight individuals including the captain, who had a non-threatening injury, and other various ranks. On the other raft were nine individuals of similar ranks.

These two life rafts, which were unable to communicate with each other, had completely different outcomes after nine days at sea awaiting rescue. On the first raft with the captain two died including the captain and all those rescued spent over a week in hospital receiving treatment. On the second raft everyone survived and all the occupants, once rescued, were back in full duty after twenty-four hours. The US Navy did some extensive research in evaluating what these two life rafts did which was so very different which produced these opposite results. It was discovered that one of the primary reasons for the second life raft to survive so successfully was the attitude that the nine servicemen, of similar ranks to the first life raft, decided from the word go. They agreed that everything they did and thought about had to be from a position of optimism as no negativity would be tolerated by any of them. On the first raft, this condition was certainly not imposed and negative outcomes were explored and discussed frequently. When they saw sharks heading towards them, they would remind each other of the life loss suffered by other people in their position. On the second life raft when they saw the sharks heading their way, they were already deciding whether they wanted shark fin soup or a shark steak for their next meal.

I put it to you that the bottom line is as this: you have a piece of hardware installed inside you called an attitude, and you must decide what software will run on it. If this strikes a chord – and the software currently running is the wrong type – I urge you to remove it and reinstall something that will make your business and life infinitely more appealing and successful.

Motivation

For me, motivation is an engine. It's a piece of machinery that turns circles within circles and wheels within wheels, and after a while works totally on autopilot. The biggest challenge around self-motivation is deciding that you want such a self-perpetuating system in the first place. Part of the difficulty is that many of us have an inbuilt fear of success. Are you aware that the reason we give up diets, exercise and return to alcohol and cigarettes after attempting to reduce or eliminate them from our lives, is based on a sudden subconscious realisation that we're going to be successful and therefore will be changing the nature of who we are? In this respect, the idea of having something that continually drives you in a positive vein can be quite alarming from a subconscious perspective.

One way I get great satisfaction through self-motivation is setting myself at least three achievable targets every day. I highly recommend this rather simple yet extraordinary habit. When you begin your business day, jot down three things that are highly achievable which you will be one hundred percent completing on that day. Write them in your diary or on a sheet of paper that you could pin to your computer screen or laptop. But wait, there's something else. Now write down one more item which has a large circle around it. Within the circle write down something which is not so easily achievable, yet something that would really make your day if you were to achieve it.

When people keep asking me what I'm excited about I have to smile inside, and then decide how I'm going to explain my circle goal of the day! You see, the act of writing down and circling something which will make a big difference to you creates a programme in your subconscious where there wasn't one before. Whereas I would take a dim view of myself not achieving the three achievable goals, the fourth-circle goal is the one that makes me feel warm inside at the end of the day when I go home to my family, pour a glass of red wine or chilled fruit juice and toast my successful day with the most important people in my life. Of course, if my circle goal fails to happen, guess what – it will be there circled yet again the following day and the next, and the one after that *until* I achieve it. It's also the most motivational feeling when I achieve my circle goal day after day. I can never understand why people take drugs when you can produce the most magical feelings inside your mind and body purely through natural pursuits whilst enjoying the feeling of elation and motivation through the heights of personal achievement.

The other way of creating this motivational engine inside you, as mentioned in an earlier chapter, is to regularly write down the things that you want to achieve as if they've already happened and then read these future goals at least once if not three times a day. There is no question that 'thoughts become things'. What you most think about eventually becomes something you believe to be true which in turn materialises before your very eyes. Therefore it's entirely sensible to seek the right type of inspiration, choose the right type of attitude and finally live with the right type of regular motivation on your journey to exceptional results.

When I first decided to write this book, some of my friends and colleagues enquired about the nature of its contents. When I threw the question back at them and asked them what they would imagine the material to be the response was more along the lines of a textbook – something that people might dip into whilst studying for their MBA and so on. As you can see in this particular chapter, I've not discussed business concepts at all. In fact many of the chapters are conceptual rather than business factual. Even though I run a very successful business, and as each month of trading goes by its inherent value improves and grows, the essence of my message in these various chapters can relate to anything in life. I decided on using it as an entrepreneur in a business context as I thought it would be an efficient vehicle for the success I wished to achieve.

I would remind anyone reading this who hasn't got their own business, nor the desire to set one up, that they may consider themselves an entrepreneur in their life as a whole, because the other thing that I learned many moons ago is that when we are born, we are born as entrepreneurs and if we continue to think as entrepreneurs we end up achieving the most amazing things. It's at that moment we decide to relinquish our entrepreneur status and choose to become employed by our life, that we join the masses of individuals who go through life's journey only to be deeply disappointed and sometimes completely shocked by their lack of personal achievement.

**Don't wait for your ship to come in –
swim out to it.**

13

Words of Wisdom?

Sitting nursing a drink surrounded by a number of business associates at a Christmas function recently, someone turned to me and looked at me squarely in the eyes asking the question, "Michael, I have to ask you something. What makes you so successful?" I blinked for a moment wondering if this was tongue in cheek and they were actually pulling my leg.

"I mean, it seems only yesterday you were talking about your new business, *Results Financial,* and here we are a few years later with everything in place making an annual profit that I'd saw my right arm off for. So what's your secret?"

Once I had established this was a serious question I realised this person was asking me for more than a confirmation of the obvious. They wanted an insight into what was not staring them readily in the face.

Of course as far as I'm concerned there are no secrets and yet when I encounter other businesses which are struggling to keep their heads above water, I do wonder why they're not doing what I often regard as 'the obvious'. In order not to make any assumptions let me share the obvious with you as we conclude this short journey.

Learn from great masters of industry

Coming from a financial services background I've evolved, both personally and from a business perspective, by seeing how other successful people have done it, something that started on my very first day in the industry.

In the 1980s, for example, there were 350,000 advisers in financial services in the UK either full or part-time. Today there are approximately only 58,000. Then it was common practice to attend events often hosted by the Life Insurance Association or LIA and listen to successful salespeople. I've never given up on this obvious little secret and only recently picked up Joseph A Michelli's book entitled *The Starbucks Experience*. What a great read – and so inspirational. Why more businesspeople are not doing the obvious escapes me. Positive input from those who have achieved great things is not only highly motivating; it's also very instructional, provided you are prepared to translate and transform an idea that may have been used by an international company into an idea you can use in your own smaller enterprise.

I remember once standing in a bookshop with a business associate who ran his own small business and he was watching me purchase a couple of business books with a wry smile on his face. He said something on the lines of "If you don't know it now, you never will," to which I replied, "When you start thinking like that about building a business, it may be time to get yourself a job".

The world is rapidly changing, at a speed greater than ever before. In fact, I have it on good authority that there have never been so many businesses on the planet at any other point in time, yet one disturbing fact is that the number of businesses that crash and burn – even after a few initial successful years – is still staggeringly high. You would think that entrepreneurs with little experience would want to gain more knowledge and experience from those businesses doing well and who are also prepared at the same time to share their good knowledge. When I buy a business book, CD or DVD, all I want is one good idea that will make that purchase a fantastic investment. It is vital to keep an open mind and never lose sight of the fact that the day you close your mind to learning from others is also the day you may as well close your business as it's unlikely to thrive without fresh original and regular external input.

Treating others as you would want to be treated

From a very early age I always remember my parents reminding me that if I was prepared to treat other people the way I'd love to be treated myself, it would be most likely that I would go on to bigger and better things in my lifetime. I make it a professional business practice for example to always take sales calls and give salespeople the opportunity to pitch their ideas to me.

I'm often staggered when I hear of small businesses that refuse to take sales calls knowing that once upon a time they were in full-time selling themselves and often found it difficult to get through to decision-makers. Maybe these individuals got some perverse pleasure from getting their own back and behaving the very way they used to detest others doing when the tables were reversed. Naturally, I'm not suggesting that I buy everything that people want to sell me; in fact I will only buy from those people who are good enough to find a requirement and then present a case where it's very difficult to say anything other than "yes".

I also extend this philosophy to helping other people in business, and sometimes even competitors. If a competitor was in trouble and needed some help to make a sale, why wouldn't I assist if I was in a strong position to do so?

Strangely enough this also applies to silly things that perhaps may appear somewhat unscientific but are most certainly connected up with this whole philosophy. For example, driving your car often means needing to get out of side roads into large streams of traffic. Curious, isn't it, how I never ever have a problem with this. People always let me out, much to the surprise of other passengers travelling with me who indicate that they've never received such volumes of courtesy on the road. When I enquire into their own driving habits and manners I soon learn that they are of the opinion that it's 'dog eat dog' on the road and they blatantly admit that they will only give way if they have to. No surprise then is it that I have this constant desire to help anyone I can in their journey and even on occasions when I may be in danger of making myself late in the process. In the East it's called karma; in the West I would refer to it as cause and effect. What you put out will always come back.

Making a difference

Whether it be a client, a member of my team or a complete stranger, I always get tremendous satisfaction and delight from making a difference in a face-to-face meeting, over the telephone or by some other communication like email. Making a difference or the 'MAD factor' has invariably produced highly tangible results for me personally as well in business.

Clients and customers are not used to a business going above and beyond the call of duty, as it were, and we all know that it doesn't take much to be able to do this regularly for your customer base. Perhaps what is even more lacking is going down the same road when looking after your team. If you're not careful you can take them for granted and it's the *people* that make the business; without them you simply have an unfulfilled dream.

Apparently, human motivation falls into three main areas: firstly, the tangible and financial; secondly, respect and recognition from others; and lastly, making a difference in your life where you intrinsically feel life is worth living and you are putting in something that gives you a buzz at the same time. It's this third area – the MAD area as I referred to before – that the majority of people put on top of their list of motivating factors. Below this comes respect and recognition, and, surprisingly, least motivating of the three areas is money and tangibles. We all know lots of well-known people who have plenty of wealth yet are sadly lacking in respect and recognition and are not doing things sufficiently in the right direction to attain that wonderful feeling of *making a difference.*

Gratitude and thanks

The other thing that can make a big difference is being grateful for what you have. This is not just about thanking people whenever you can; it's about realising what you have and enjoying the moment in celebration. There was a time when I used to live outside the moment. Many entrepreneurs do this. Whatever they're doing, their mind is on the next thing.

So for example, during the day they are thinking about having a meal with their partner rather than on the job in hand and when the evening arrives and they are sitting at the dinner table having this wonderful meal, their mind is on being in work again the next morning and what they have to do. Living outside the moment means you are behaving in an ungrateful way for what life has given you. The only way you can really appreciate and be grateful for what you have is to live and enjoy each moment and accept it for what it is rather than always looking one step ahead.

One of the main reasons why I watch the news on television

or read about current events in the newspapers is to continually remind myself how fortunate I am compared with other poor souls who are being challenged, often in sad and dramatic ways.

Being grateful is not about losing your ambition for success. It's about shoring up your position in the present day in order to build a stronger and even more exciting future.

The away-day

From time to time I cancel all meetings and take the day off and spend the day with myself. This 'away-day' idea allows me to be creative, thoughtful and delightfully provocative about what's in store, both in business and personally. When is the last time you had an away-day? When did you take yourself away when no one could reach you and spend a good eight hours having a meeting with yourself? Once again, all I require is one really good sound idea in spending such time for it to be entirely worthwhile and a great time investment.

You don't need to do this every week or indeed every month, but you might want to consider it at least once a quarter, or when you feel you need to get off the journey and have a rest and think about where you are and where you're headed.

Time isn't money

You will be familiar with the well-worn phrase 'time is money'. Nothing could be further from the truth. You can never ever equate time with money, as they are two totally different commodities with completely opposing value. Money is replaceable. It can be created, spent without guilt. It can be saved and invested as you desire. Time on the other hand is surely your most precious asset. It cannot be saved in the same way money can. You can't collect it for the future, and it's disappearing second by second in your life.

If you equate time with money then you are placing some sort of value on your time. May I suggest that time cannot have a value attached, given that you have no idea how much you currently have allotted to your name. If it was a saleable commodity you would be completely mad to sell any of it, not knowing the resource you have in the first place. This whole approach and attitude towards time is one that I have to keep reminding myself about. It irritates me when people keep me waiting as I see them stealing from me and if I'm ever late for any event I do my utmost to ensure that other people's time is not wasted as a result and in the event of me really messing up, I then make it my business to somehow compensate for the situation that has arisen.

We live in a life where everyone is an individual and so unique that no one else on the planet shares our fingerprints, our exact looks, our precise age and birthplace and certainly not our exact beliefs, ambitions and future dreams. We are all born special, and if other people recognise you as such it must mean you are doing something right. Equally, if you rarely get a comment like this and you don't feel particularly special, it's never too late.

As I mentioned earlier in the book, one of my favourite films of all time, which I would strongly recommend you see if you haven't already done so, is *Dead Poets Society*. In the film, Robin Williams plays a teacher who teaches a group of schoolboys the magic of thinking outside the box. Particularly interesting is the way he extols the precious value of time. I leave you with the Latin phrase that's been around for at least two thousand years 'carpe diem' or *seize the day*. Before you do that, however, you must seize your mind and seize the thoughts that run through it on a day-by-day basis, because if you can control your thoughts you'll control your mind, which in turn will help you make the most of every day and as a result help you make the most of your life. If you're an entrepreneur, this also must mean business success.

Here's wishing you every continued success.

Michael Bell